The Mindful Nature Connection Journal

Copyright © 2020 Clare Snowdon
ISBN 9798587561274

Introduction

This journal is intended to help you connect more deeply with nature and also with yourself – your true self, and the whole spectrum of your life experiences – the fun, the awe-inspiring, as well as the challenges we get to learn from.

The prompts are given as guides only, you can use these pages in any way that feels right for you. Your relationships and experiences will be unique to you. I hope that these prompts help to give you a different perspective and to help cultivate a relationship with nature that helps both you and the huge variety of beings we share this planet with.

I have also included a few nature connection and mindfulness practices you might like to try. I have plenty of examples, including a 30 day challenge on my website at www.dragonmindfulness.co.uk You can find videos of many of these on my YouTube channel https://www.youtube.com/user/calliegs/videos as well as audio guidance on my Soundcloud channel https://soundcloud.com/clare-snowdon-1

I have completed the first page of the journal to give you an idea of some of the things you could write (or draw)!

Journaling helps me to notice more. It encourages me to get outside and to pay attention. It prompts me to reflect and consider things more carefully. Lots of the fun and insights from keeping a journal are found in going back and reading past entries. I can see when the daffodil shoots appeared last year or when the swifts returned to Africa. In part it is a scientific record, possibly showing changes in the local climate, but it is also very much about the physical, emotional and spiritual elements of my experience.

Many of the journal sections are an invitation to notice patterns and seasonal changes. Just getting outside to note how the weather is or if you can see the moon is a first step to getting back in touch with nature in the way that our ancestors would.

In the sightings section you could simply have a list of different species, habitats, rocks etc or you could focus on giving more detail about, for example, a particular bird you saw and how it was behaving. This is an opportunity to get to know your neighbours! You might like to learn the names of a handful of the most common birds, trees or plants in your area if you do not already know them.

I have included some nature connection activities you could try, but there are many more possibilities for you to explore. It does not have to be anything formal. The key is to pay attention, using your senses.

Getting creative is a great way to connect with nature – drawing, taking photos, writing poems or stories, or even dancing or making music. I also like to express gratitude and look for ways I can help nature. This might be signing a petition, raising awareness of environmental issues or helping a charity, or something more practical like creating a wildlife garden, planting seeds for pollinators etc. I have included a whole page for this.

However you use this journal, I wish you many happy adventures, filled with joy and wonder!

Seven Nature Connection Ideas

1. *Breathing with Trees*

Nature connection is not just about your outer experience. It is also about recognising that you are nature through your inner experience - both within your body and through your consciousness.

Breathing is the most fundamental process of nature which occurs within our bodies - from the instant we take our first breath and every moment of our lives afterwards. It is part of a whole host of processes - electrical signals from the brain and the movement of muscles, which feed into all sorts of activity within your body, through your blood and heart to virtually every cell. You do not need to understand it or control it - it is all taken care of for you.

It also connects you with the outer world. So the invitation is to breathe with a tree - it can be standing next to a tree or plant or by simply visualising a tree or plant (or plankton/algae if that has more meaning for you - you can even experiment with this and see how it is to connect with each - real tree vs visualised tree and land plants vs plankton)! Every breath you take in contains oxygen, provided by trees, plants and algae. Every time you exhale, you breathe out carbon dioxide, which the trees and plankton need to complete their cycle of photosynthesis.

As you breathe in, connect with the sensations of the breath - perhaps visualising drawing the gift of oxygen from nature into your body and spreading to every cell. As you breathe out, noticing again the sensations of the body and perhaps imagining it as a gift back to the tree (or other life form that you are connecting with).

2. *The Weather Station*

The inspiration for this practice came from working with people who spent most of their time outdoors. I was amazed by their ability to read the clues and signs of the world around them, predicting the weather with incredible accuracy. It turns out that most of us have this ability, but we have lost our connection to our senses and the world around us. The good news is that we can rediscover it.

So, the idea for this exercise is to tune in to your body and your senses (possibly more than the 5 common ones - it might even be interesting to explore what senses you use and whether you find new ones you did not know about).

It is always a good idea to start with a few moments just arriving - letting go of to-do lists etc. and bringing your awareness to your breath and your body - possibly just noticing the stillness in your body for a minute or two.

Then, I like to tune in to the sensations on my body of the air temperature, noticing if it feels the same everywhere or if different parts of the body feel warmer or cooler. You could then notice if there is any movement of the air around you and whether this is changeable. Are you able to detect the humidity of the air? Perhaps it is raining - if so, you might like to take note of any judgement and feelings you have around this and possibly experiment with releasing the judgements, just seeing how rain is before you attach any labels or thoughts about it. There are lots of different types of rain, so perhaps you could explore what kind of rain it is and any sounds or other effects it makes (bubbles and ripples in the puddles perhaps). Next, you might notice the quality of the light. Are you able to tell what time of day it is?

Finally, noticing any clouds. What are these like? Are they moving? What do you think the weather will be like in the next hour or the next day?

3. *Tree Connection*

I was first inspired to do this practice after I leant against a large conifer to cool down after a run. I noticed that I felt supported by the tree and got curious about this. During challenging times, I would lean against a tree in the garden and share (mentally) that I was finding things hard. It really helped to feel held, accepted, and supported at a time I couldn't be with loved ones. So, you may like to try this for yourself. Another approach is to perhaps take a woodland walk and ask yourself "if this tree had a character or personality, what would it be?" Then just allow the answers to come from your felt experience. It is a genuinely lovely way to connect with nature.

4. *Touch and Textures*

This is about exploring with your hands and eyes. Simply feel different textures - really paying attention to the sensations in your hands (i.e. staying with the direct experience rather than analysing it). Perhaps there is an emotional quality associated with the texture - warm and inviting, bold, protective etc. Obviously not all textures like to be touched - stinging nettles for example so be careful not to touch anything that might be an irritant. However, you can explore these textures using your eyes to look and see what they might feel like.

5. *Tree Symphony*

Trees are like musical instruments, played by the wind. Each tree has its own characteristic sound - the beech tree is different from the aspen and so on. Trees also sound different depending on the landscape and how they are spaced. So, the invitation is to explore this for yourself, whether you can find a single tree or a whole woodland - just get curious with the sounds.

6. *Sky Watching*

Looking at the sky can be very therapeutic. You are invited to watch the clouds, the stars, birds, insects or other airborne nature! If it is appropriate, you might like to lie on the ground on your back and look up (you may need something waterproof underneath you and a blanket to make this feasible). It is lovely to feel the earth beneath you and the sky above and you get a very different perspective from the one you might normally have. It is, of course, fine to do this standing or sitting too.

7. *Scent Hunt*

This is a bit like a scavenger hunt but without the list. The idea is to get out and find as many different scents as you can. You can go for scents you know to find - e.g. herbs etc. as well as exploring whether other things have a smell that perhaps you hadn't noticed before.

Journal pages

<u>Example</u>

Date *Monday December 28th 2020*

Sunrise *watched before sunrise. Pale blue sky with reddish tinge, a little birdsong, crisp air*

Sunset *1600*

Moon phase *waxing gibbous. Looked at the moon last night in clear sky – like greeting a dear friend!*

Weather (hot, cold, humid, dry, precipitation, clouds, wind etc.) *Frosty, cold, crisp, clear skies, no wind. Feels like a perfect winter day. Pond has iced over. Clouded over later – fuzzy clouds – I ought to learn the different names!*

Signs of the seasons *Frost! Snow in Wales apparently. Storm Bella yesterday but was calm here by midday, with clear skies and sunshine – total contrast. Daffodil shoots appearing. Holly berries.*

Sightings/connections (birds, plants, trees, animals, natural features) *Parakeets, starlings, crows, robin, blue tits, great tits, sparrows, wood pigeons, gulls, leaf buds on the apple tree*

Night Sky (stars, constellations, other – meteors, planets etc) *Saw the plough this morning but was more focused on birdsong. Hoping the skies stay clear tonight. Now regretting I did not pay more attention in case it is a missed opportunity!*

Nature connection activity (what you did, how you felt, what you noticed etc.) *The Weather Station – can see breath. Lower legs felt cold – maybe the air is colder near the ground. Something very* comforting about the frost – hard to put my finger on it, but happy to just explore the feeling without explanation!

Drawings, pictures, stories, poems, extra notes, gratitudes, ways I gave service to nature

Broke the ice on the pond to ensure nothing is trapped. Made sure the birds had enough food. Grateful for this crisp, dry weather and all the wonderful bird visitors, winter flowers. Lovely to have the time to get outdoors a few times today.

I may go online and try to find a winter poem. I wrote this one:

The Tree Beneath the Leaves

Standing here bare, unafraid

Accepting of the winter days

Take me in my current state

A resting place for crow's announcements

Grieve not for what has gone

Not swift nor swallow nor autumn's fire

Proudly set against the greys

Rejoicing in my silent dance

Here I'll stay, while all things change

Singing to your hopeful heart.

Date

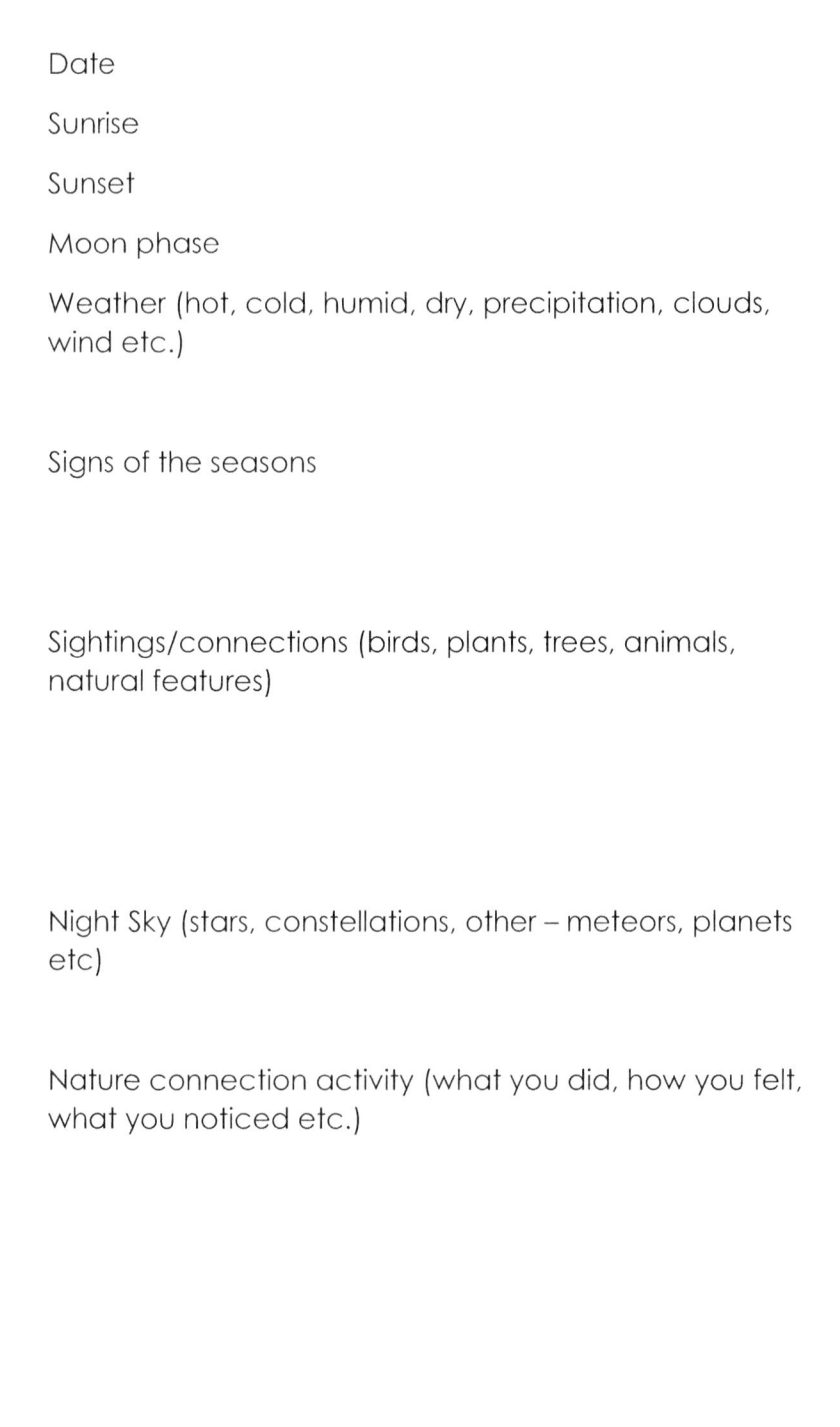

Sunrise

Sunset

Moon phase

Weather (hot, cold, humid, dry, precipitation, clouds, wind etc.)

Signs of the seasons

Sightings/connections (birds, plants, trees, animals, natural features)

Night Sky (stars, constellations, other – meteors, planets etc)

Nature connection activity (what you did, how you felt, what you noticed etc.)

Drawings, pictures, stories, poems, extra notes, gratitudes, ways I gave service to nature

Date

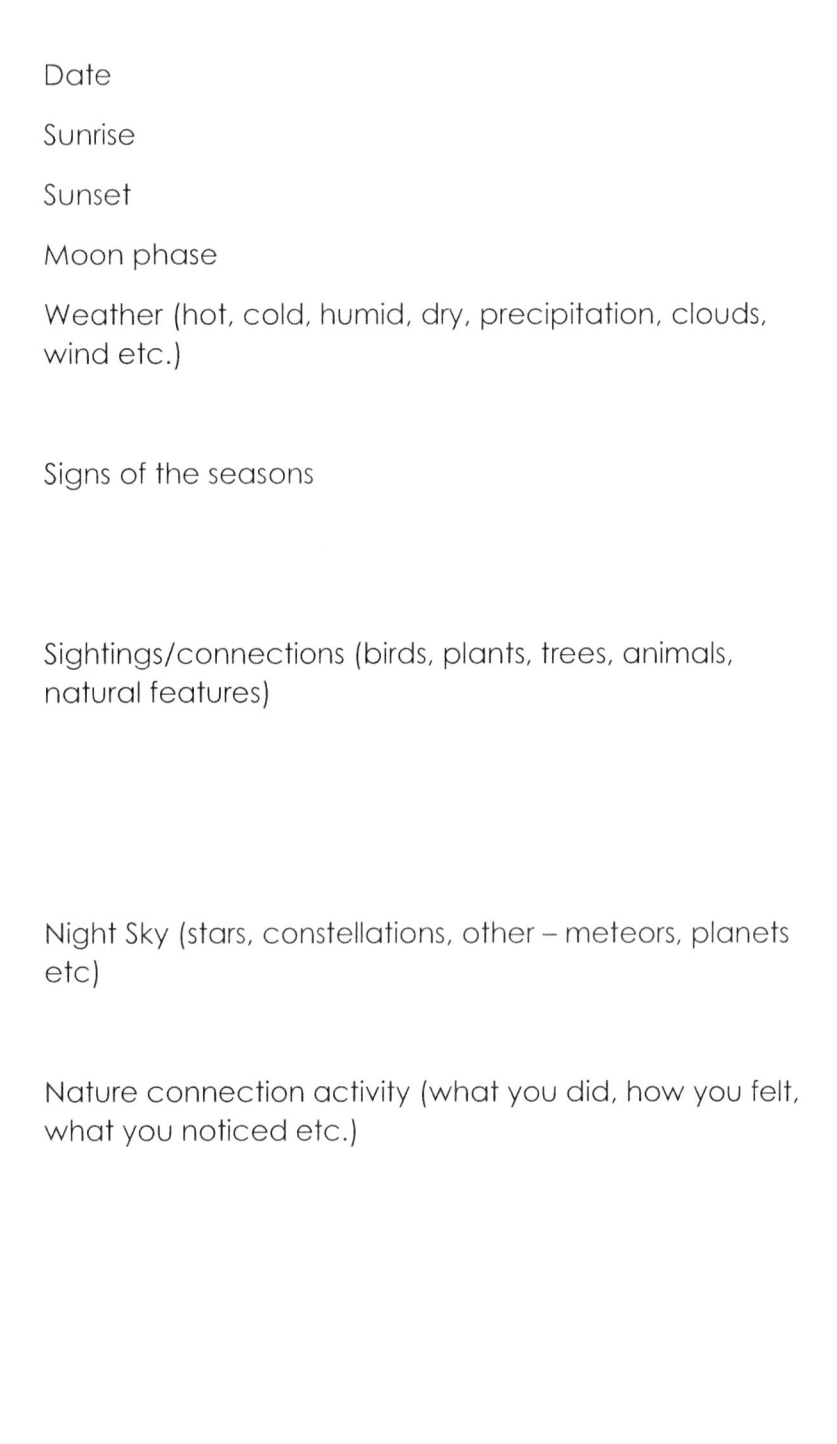

Sunrise

Sunset

Moon phase

Weather (hot, cold, humid, dry, precipitation, clouds, wind etc.)

Signs of the seasons

Sightings/connections (birds, plants, trees, animals, natural features)

Night Sky (stars, constellations, other – meteors, planets etc)

Nature connection activity (what you did, how you felt, what you noticed etc.)

Drawings, pictures, stories, poems, extra notes, gratitudes, ways I gave service to nature

Date

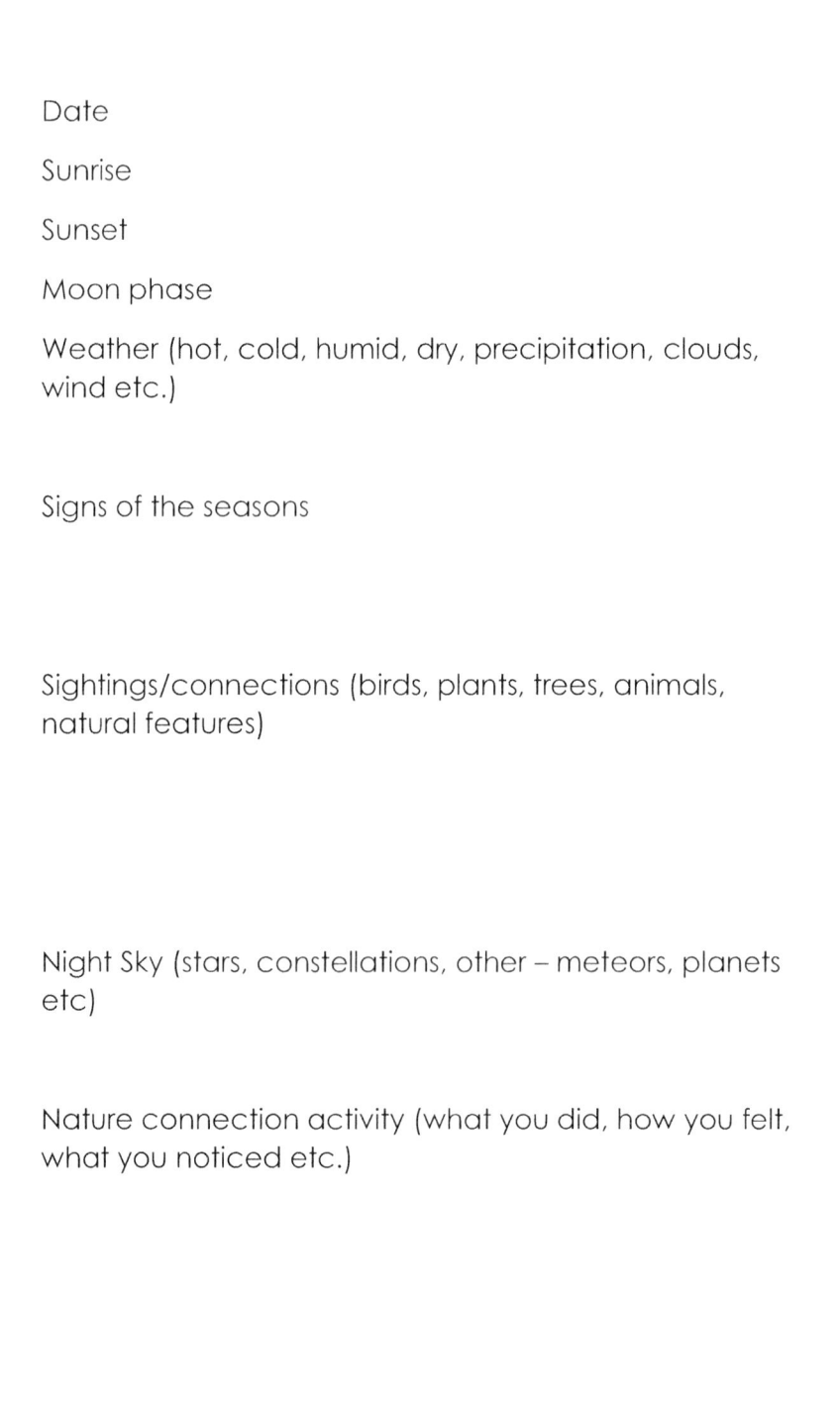

Sunrise

Sunset

Moon phase

Weather (hot, cold, humid, dry, precipitation, clouds, wind etc.)

Signs of the seasons

Sightings/connections (birds, plants, trees, animals, natural features)

Night Sky (stars, constellations, other – meteors, planets etc)

Nature connection activity (what you did, how you felt, what you noticed etc.)

Drawings, pictures, stories, poems, extra notes, gratitudes, ways I gave service to nature

Date

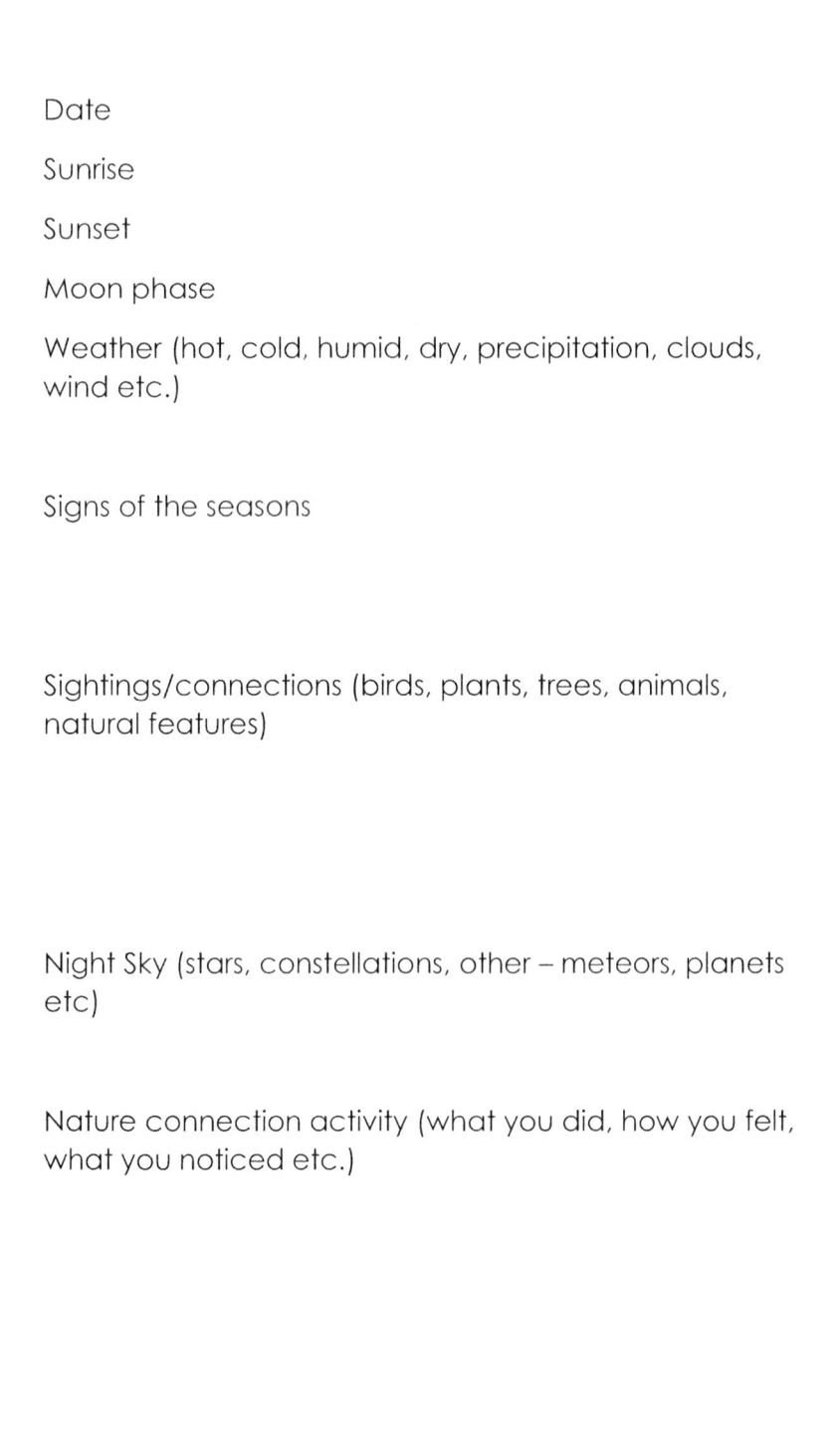

Sunrise

Sunset

Moon phase

Weather (hot, cold, humid, dry, precipitation, clouds, wind etc.)

Signs of the seasons

Sightings/connections (birds, plants, trees, animals, natural features)

Night Sky (stars, constellations, other – meteors, planets etc)

Nature connection activity (what you did, how you felt, what you noticed etc.)

Drawings, pictures, stories, poems, extra notes, gratitudes, ways I gave service to nature

Date

Sunrise

Sunset

Moon phase

Weather (hot, cold, humid, dry, precipitation, clouds, wind etc.)

Signs of the seasons

Sightings/connections (birds, plants, trees, animals, natural features)

Night Sky (stars, constellations, other – meteors, planets etc)

Nature connection activity (what you did, how you felt, what you noticed etc.)

Drawings, pictures, stories, poems, extra notes, gratitudes, ways I gave service to nature

Date

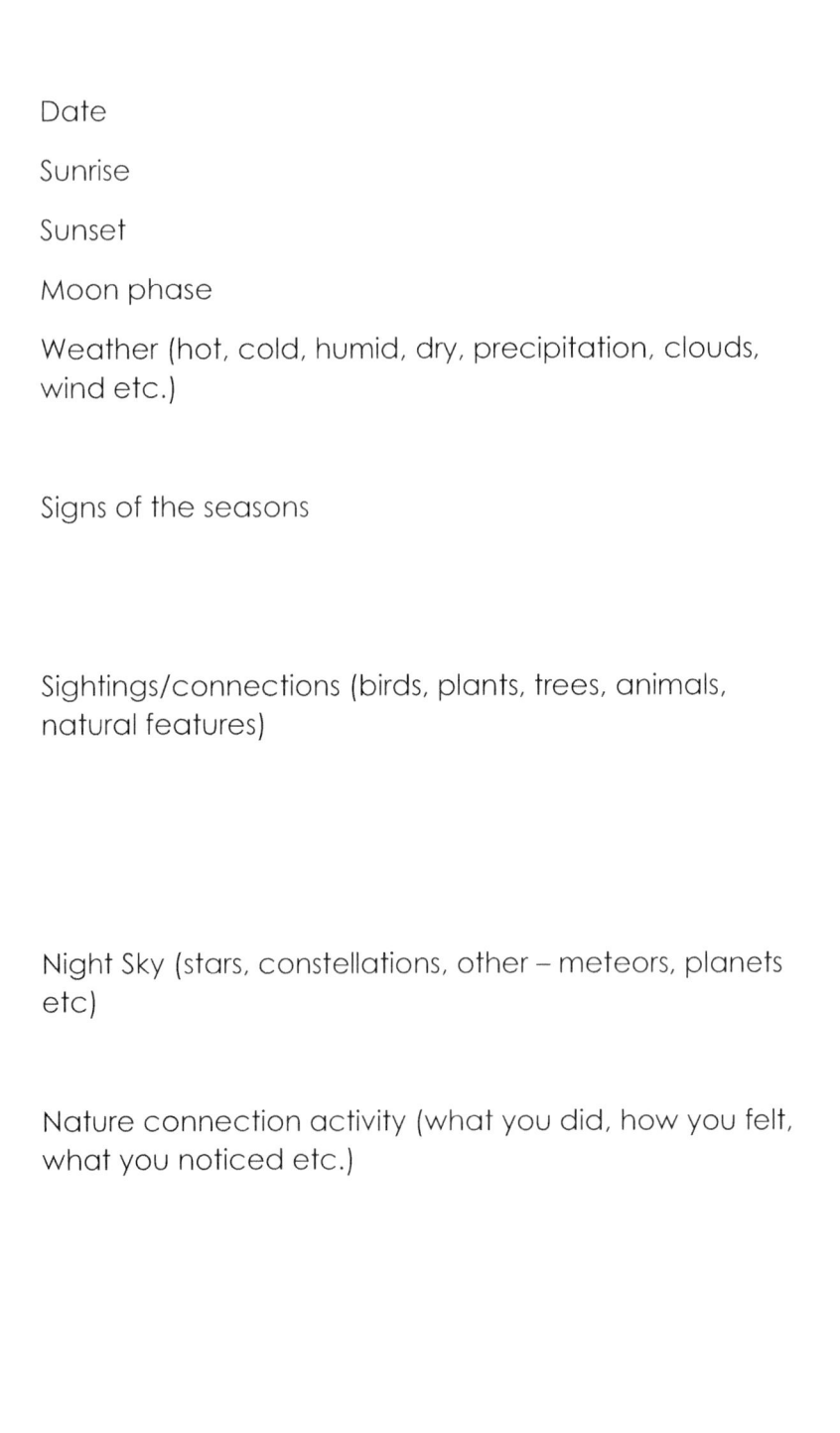

Sunrise

Sunset

Moon phase

Weather (hot, cold, humid, dry, precipitation, clouds, wind etc.)

Signs of the seasons

Sightings/connections (birds, plants, trees, animals, natural features)

Night Sky (stars, constellations, other – meteors, planets etc)

Nature connection activity (what you did, how you felt, what you noticed etc.)

Drawings, pictures, stories, poems, extra notes, gratitudes, ways I gave service to nature

Date

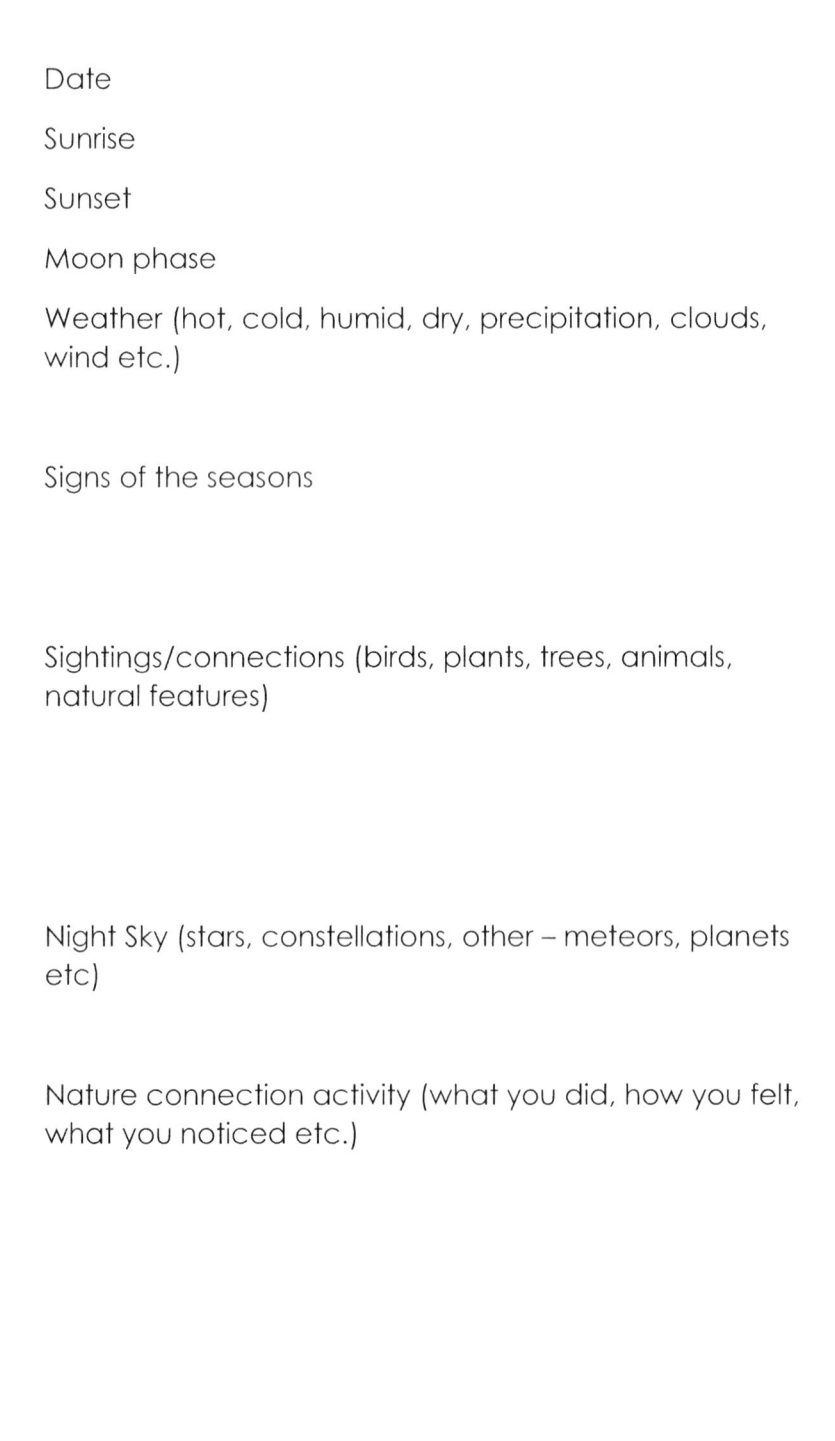

Sunrise

Sunset

Moon phase

Weather (hot, cold, humid, dry, precipitation, clouds, wind etc.)

Signs of the seasons

Sightings/connections (birds, plants, trees, animals, natural features)

Night Sky (stars, constellations, other – meteors, planets etc)

Nature connection activity (what you did, how you felt, what you noticed etc.)

Drawings, pictures, stories, poems, extra notes, gratitudes, ways I gave service to nature

Date

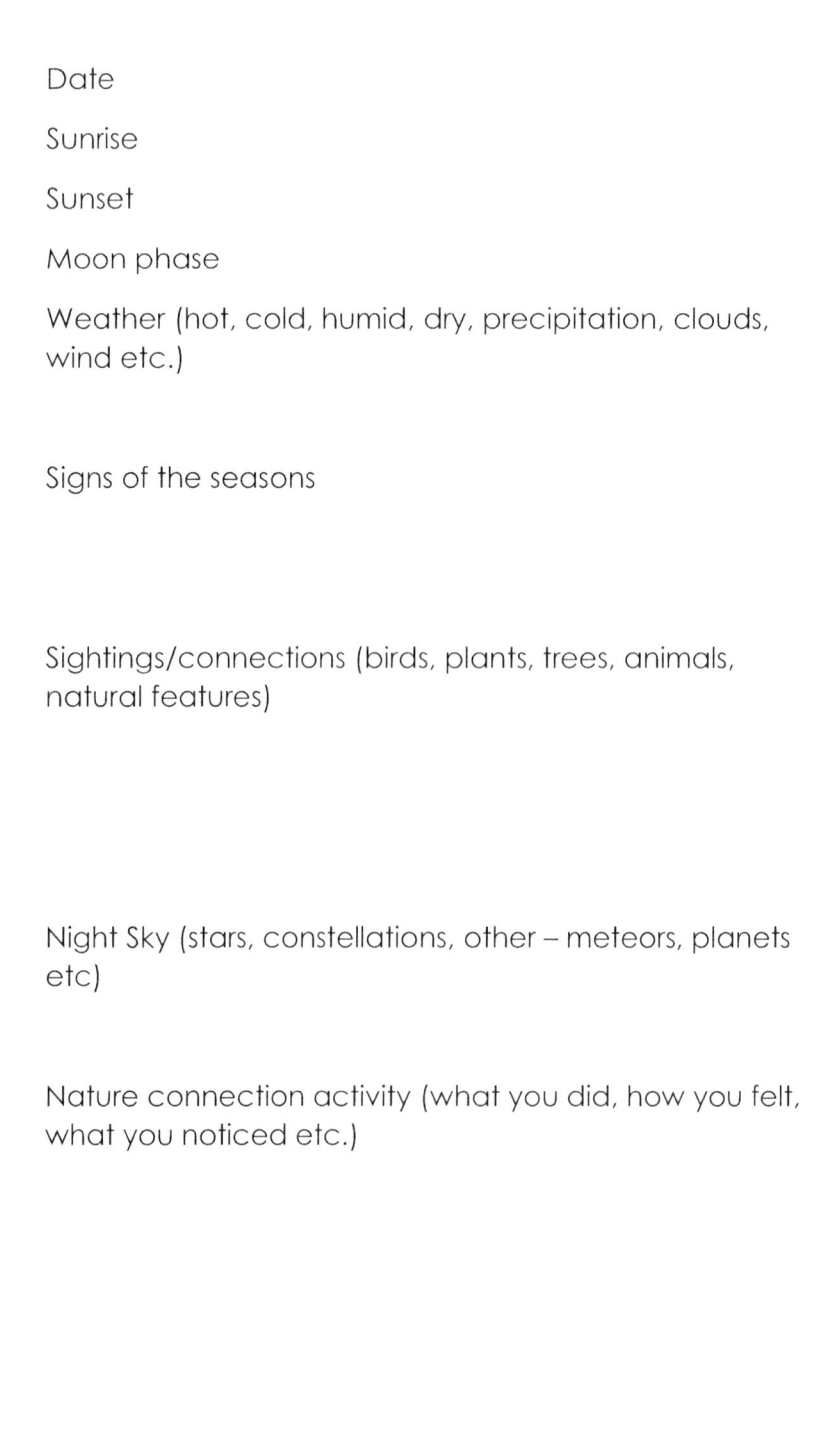

Sunrise

Sunset

Moon phase

Weather (hot, cold, humid, dry, precipitation, clouds, wind etc.)

Signs of the seasons

Sightings/connections (birds, plants, trees, animals, natural features)

Night Sky (stars, constellations, other – meteors, planets etc)

Nature connection activity (what you did, how you felt, what you noticed etc.)

Drawings, pictures, stories, poems, extra notes, gratitudes, ways I gave service to nature

Date

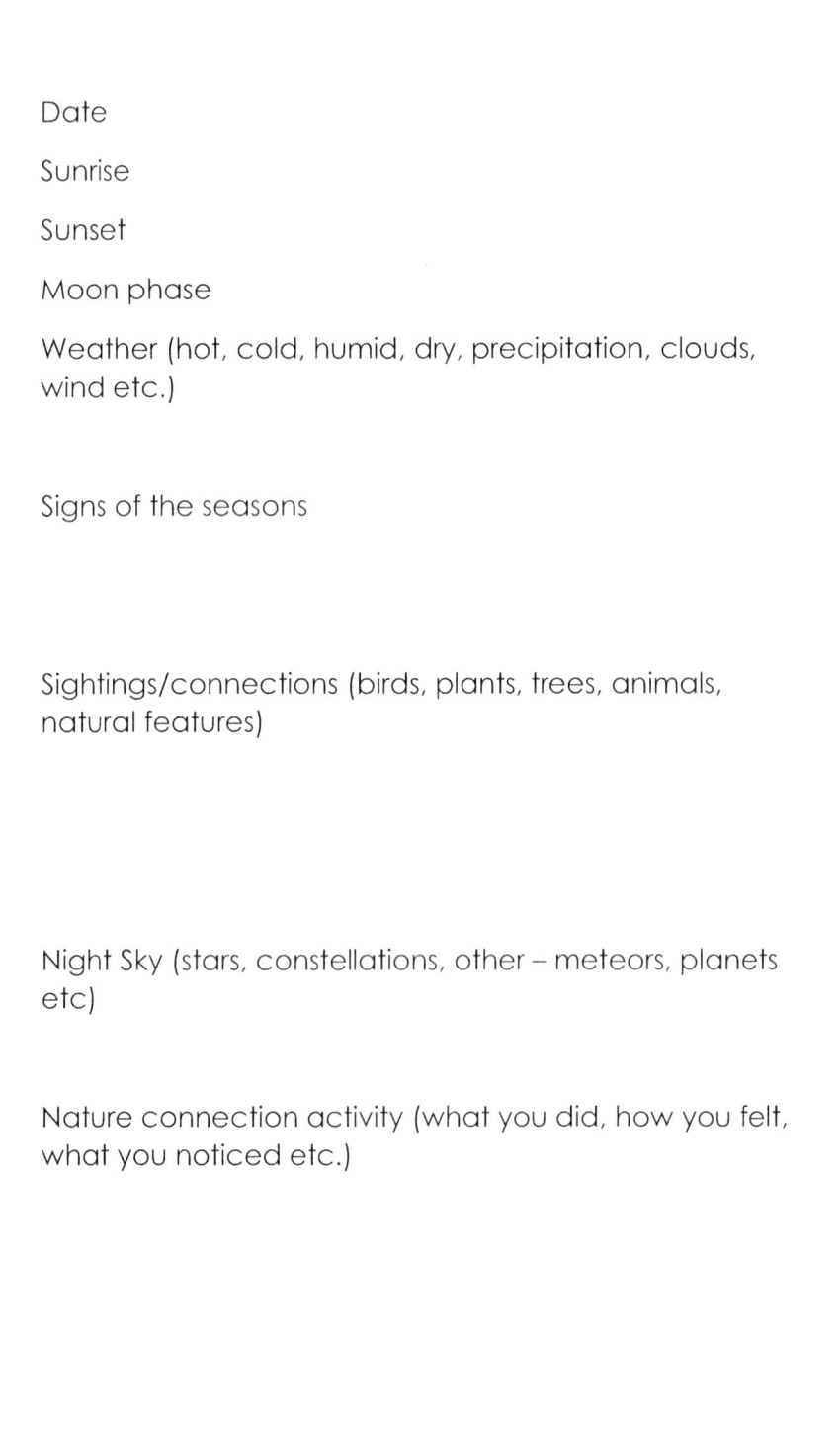

Sunrise

Sunset

Moon phase

Weather (hot, cold, humid, dry, precipitation, clouds, wind etc.)

Signs of the seasons

Sightings/connections (birds, plants, trees, animals, natural features)

Night Sky (stars, constellations, other – meteors, planets etc)

Nature connection activity (what you did, how you felt, what you noticed etc.)

Drawings, pictures, stories, poems, extra notes, gratitudes, ways I gave service to nature

Date

Sunrise

Sunset

Moon phase

Weather (hot, cold, humid, dry, precipitation, clouds, wind etc.)

Signs of the seasons

Sightings/connections (birds, plants, trees, animals, natural features)

Night Sky (stars, constellations, other – meteors, planets etc)

Nature connection activity (what you did, how you felt, what you noticed etc.)

Drawings, pictures, stories, poems, extra notes, gratitudes, ways I gave service to nature

Date

Sunrise

Sunset

Moon phase

Weather (hot, cold, humid, dry, precipitation, clouds, wind etc.)

Signs of the seasons

Sightings/connections (birds, plants, trees, animals, natural features)

Night Sky (stars, constellations, other – meteors, planets etc)

Nature connection activity (what you did, how you felt, what you noticed etc.)

Drawings, pictures, stories, poems, extra notes, gratitudes, ways I gave service to nature

Date

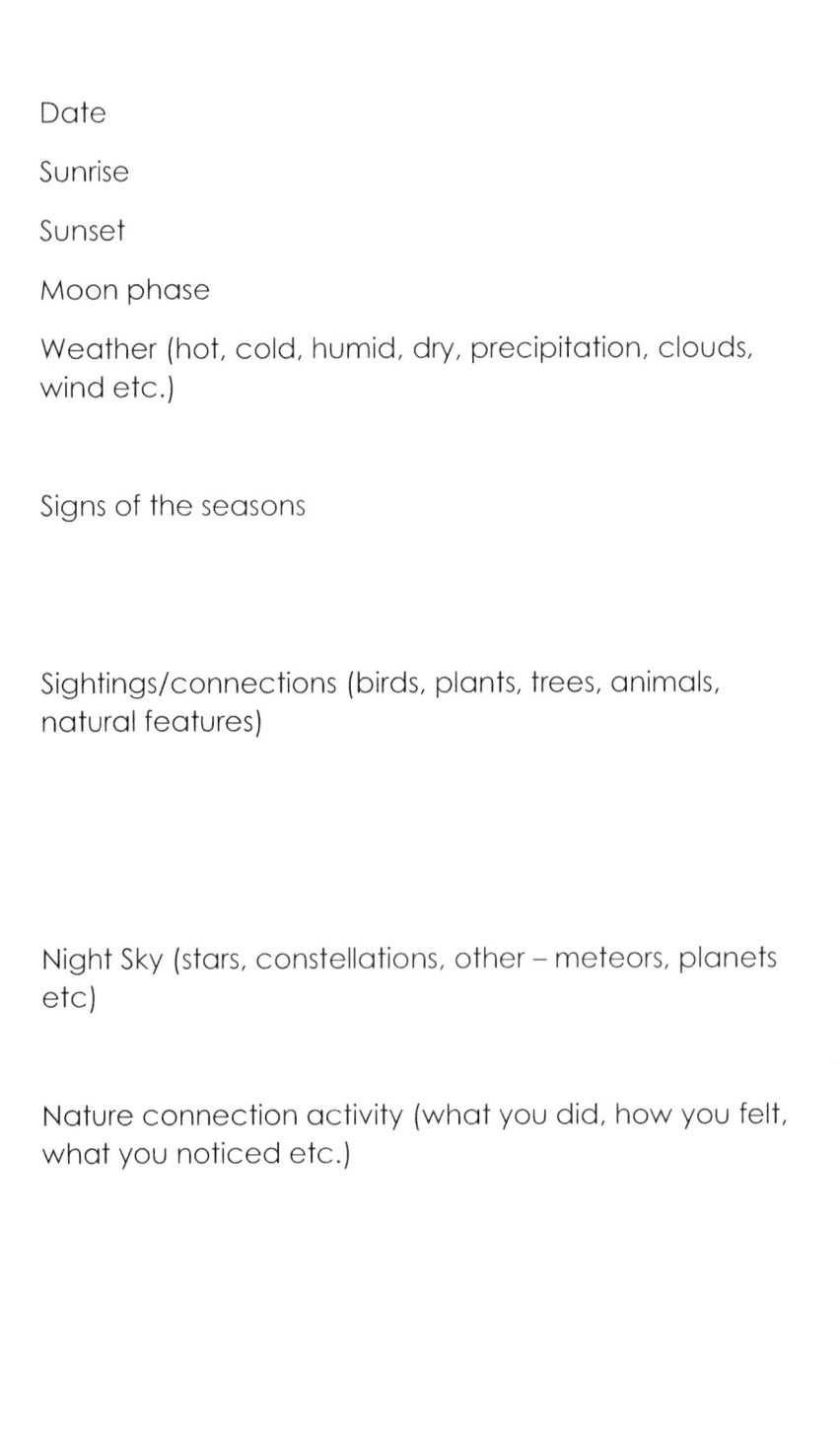

Sunrise

Sunset

Moon phase

Weather (hot, cold, humid, dry, precipitation, clouds, wind etc.)

Signs of the seasons

Sightings/connections (birds, plants, trees, animals, natural features)

Night Sky (stars, constellations, other – meteors, planets etc)

Nature connection activity (what you did, how you felt, what you noticed etc.)

Drawings, pictures, stories, poems, extra notes, gratitudes, ways I gave service to nature

Date

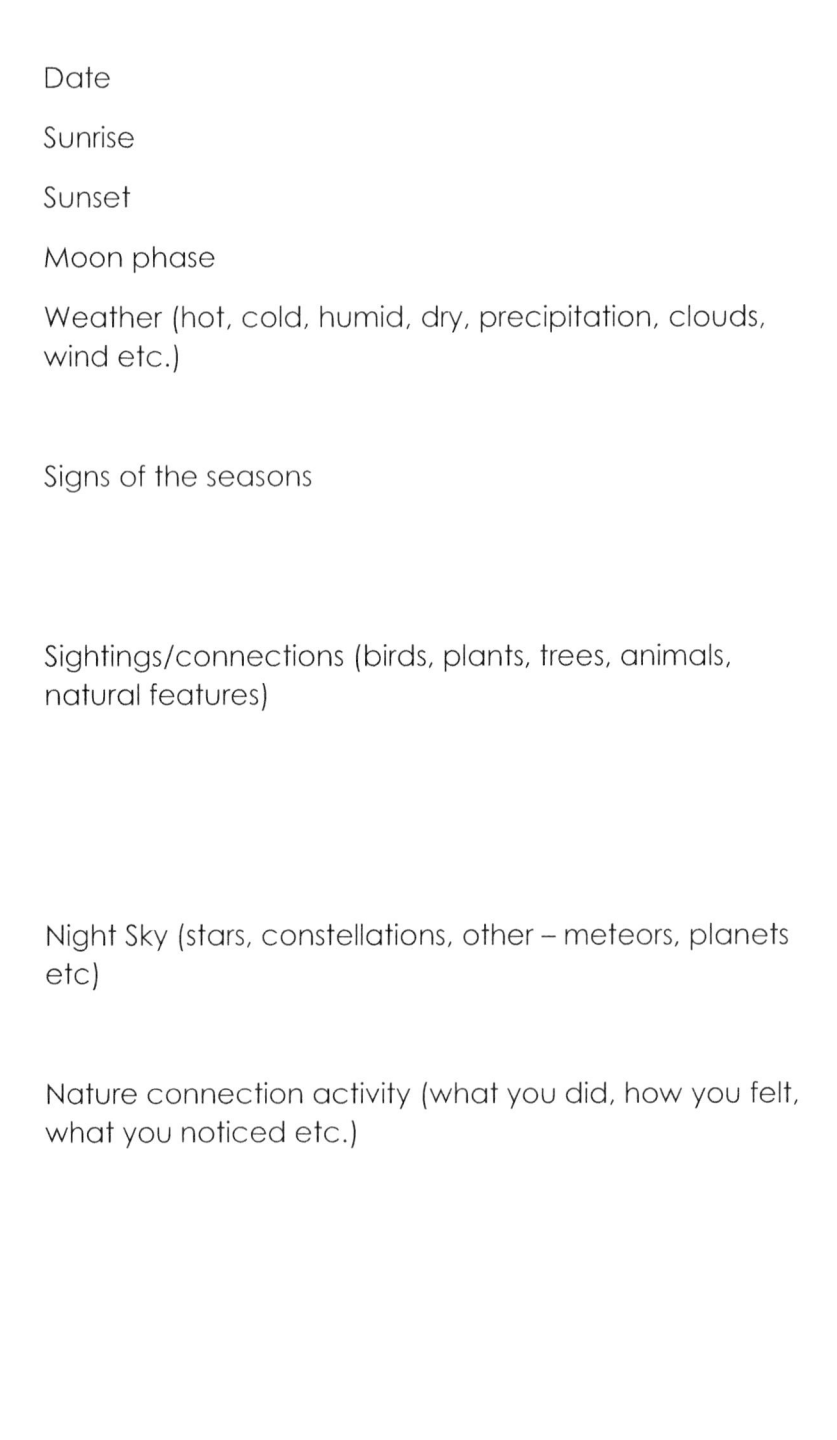

Sunrise

Sunset

Moon phase

Weather (hot, cold, humid, dry, precipitation, clouds, wind etc.)

Signs of the seasons

Sightings/connections (birds, plants, trees, animals, natural features)

Night Sky (stars, constellations, other – meteors, planets etc)

Nature connection activity (what you did, how you felt, what you noticed etc.)

Drawings, pictures, stories, poems, extra notes, gratitudes, ways I gave service to nature

Date

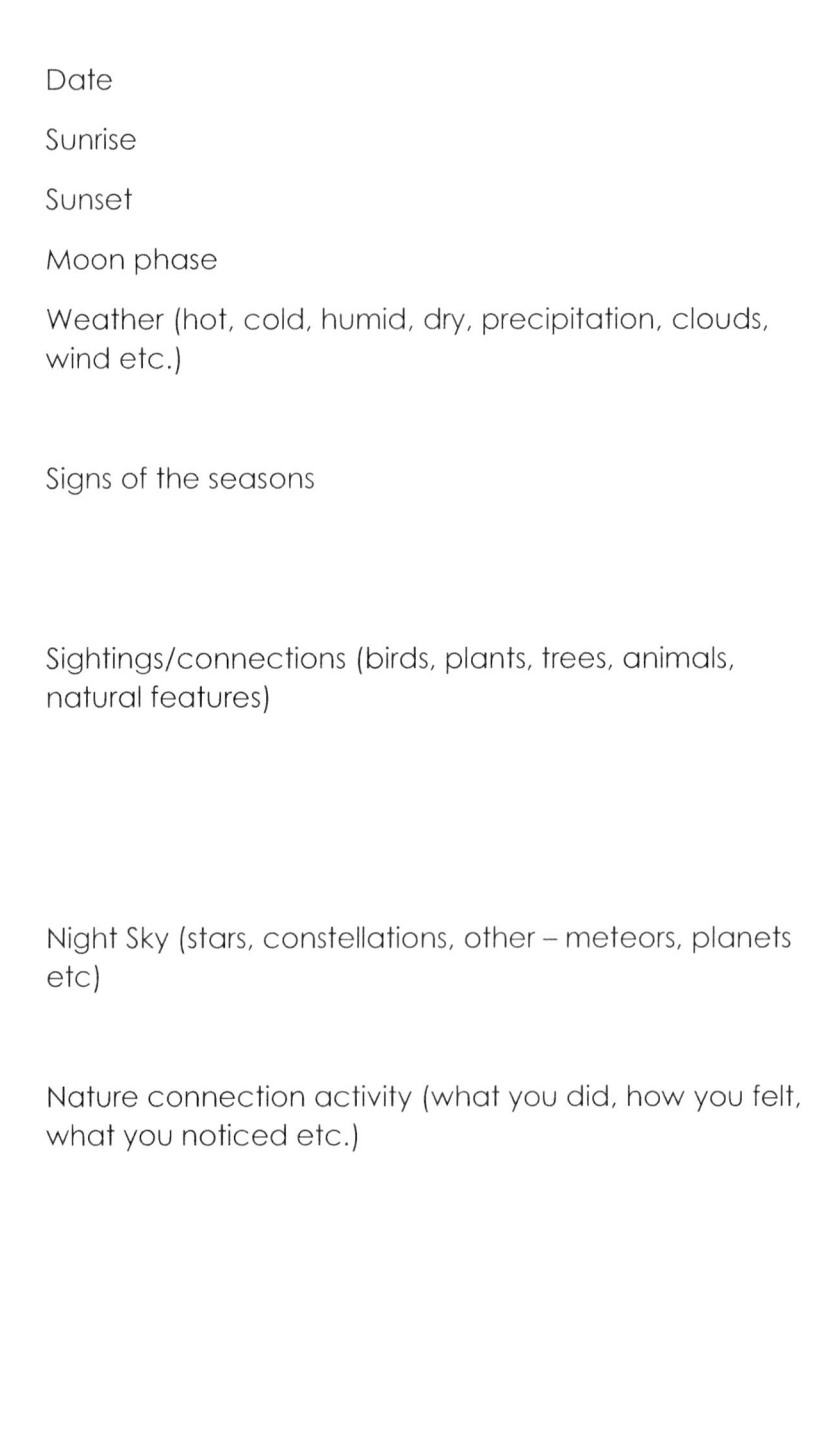

Sunrise

Sunset

Moon phase

Weather (hot, cold, humid, dry, precipitation, clouds, wind etc.)

Signs of the seasons

Sightings/connections (birds, plants, trees, animals, natural features)

Night Sky (stars, constellations, other – meteors, planets etc)

Nature connection activity (what you did, how you felt, what you noticed etc.)

Drawings, pictures, stories, poems, extra notes, gratitudes, ways I gave service to nature

Date

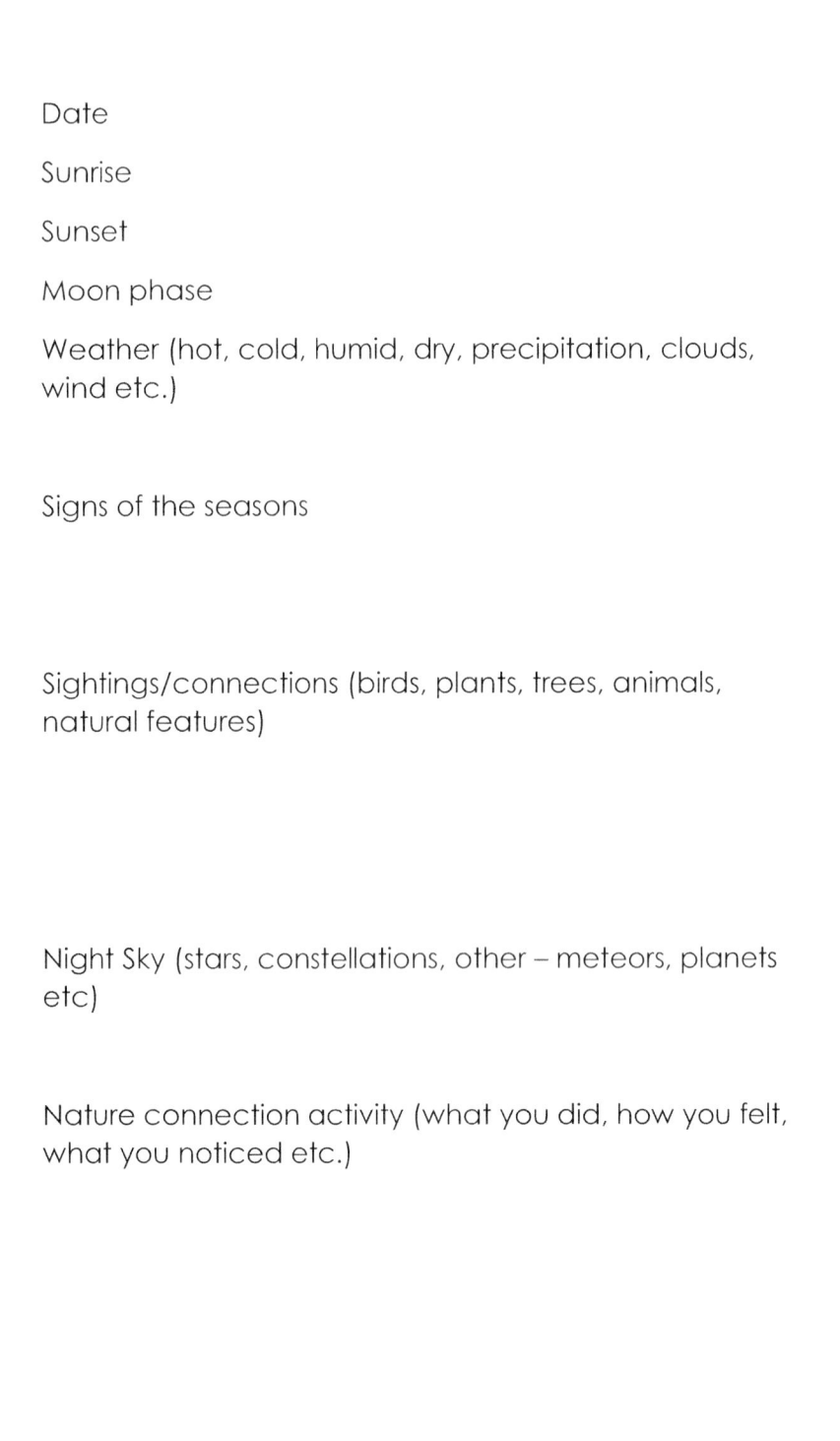

Sunrise

Sunset

Moon phase

Weather (hot, cold, humid, dry, precipitation, clouds, wind etc.)

Signs of the seasons

Sightings/connections (birds, plants, trees, animals, natural features)

Night Sky (stars, constellations, other – meteors, planets etc)

Nature connection activity (what you did, how you felt, what you noticed etc.)

Drawings, pictures, stories, poems, extra notes, gratitudes, ways I gave service to nature

Date

Sunrise

Sunset

Moon phase

Weather (hot, cold, humid, dry, precipitation, clouds, wind etc.)

Signs of the seasons

Sightings/connections (birds, plants, trees, animals, natural features)

Night Sky (stars, constellations, other – meteors, planets etc)

Nature connection activity (what you did, how you felt, what you noticed etc.)

Drawings, pictures, stories, poems, extra notes, gratitudes, ways I gave service to nature

Date

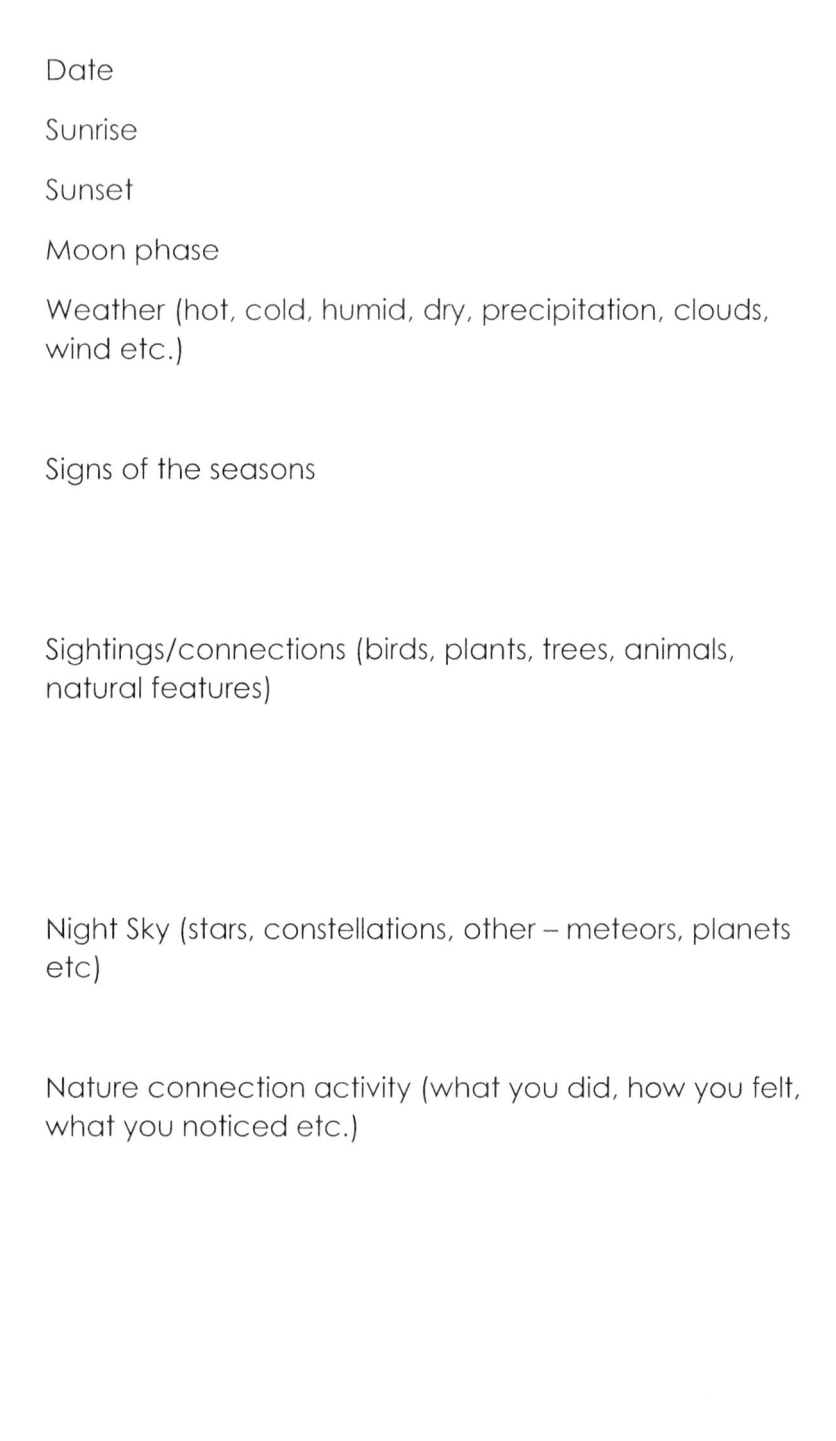

Sunrise

Sunset

Moon phase

Weather (hot, cold, humid, dry, precipitation, clouds, wind etc.)

Signs of the seasons

Sightings/connections (birds, plants, trees, animals, natural features)

Night Sky (stars, constellations, other – meteors, planets etc)

Nature connection activity (what you did, how you felt, what you noticed etc.)

Drawings, pictures, stories, poems, extra notes, gratitudes, ways I gave service to nature

Date

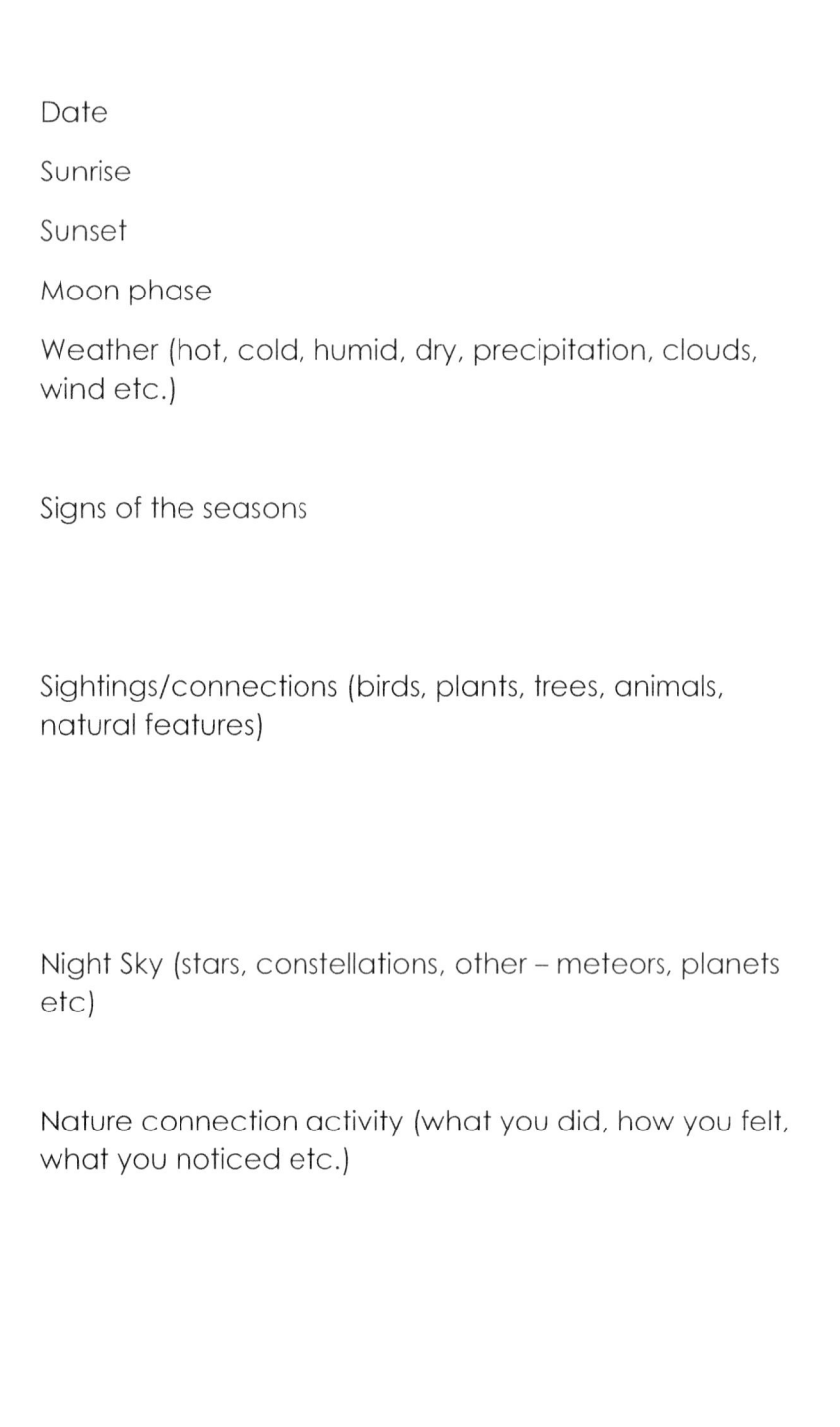

Sunrise

Sunset

Moon phase

Weather (hot, cold, humid, dry, precipitation, clouds, wind etc.)

Signs of the seasons

Sightings/connections (birds, plants, trees, animals, natural features)

Night Sky (stars, constellations, other – meteors, planets etc)

Nature connection activity (what you did, how you felt, what you noticed etc.)

Drawings, pictures, stories, poems, extra notes, gratitudes, ways I gave service to nature

Date

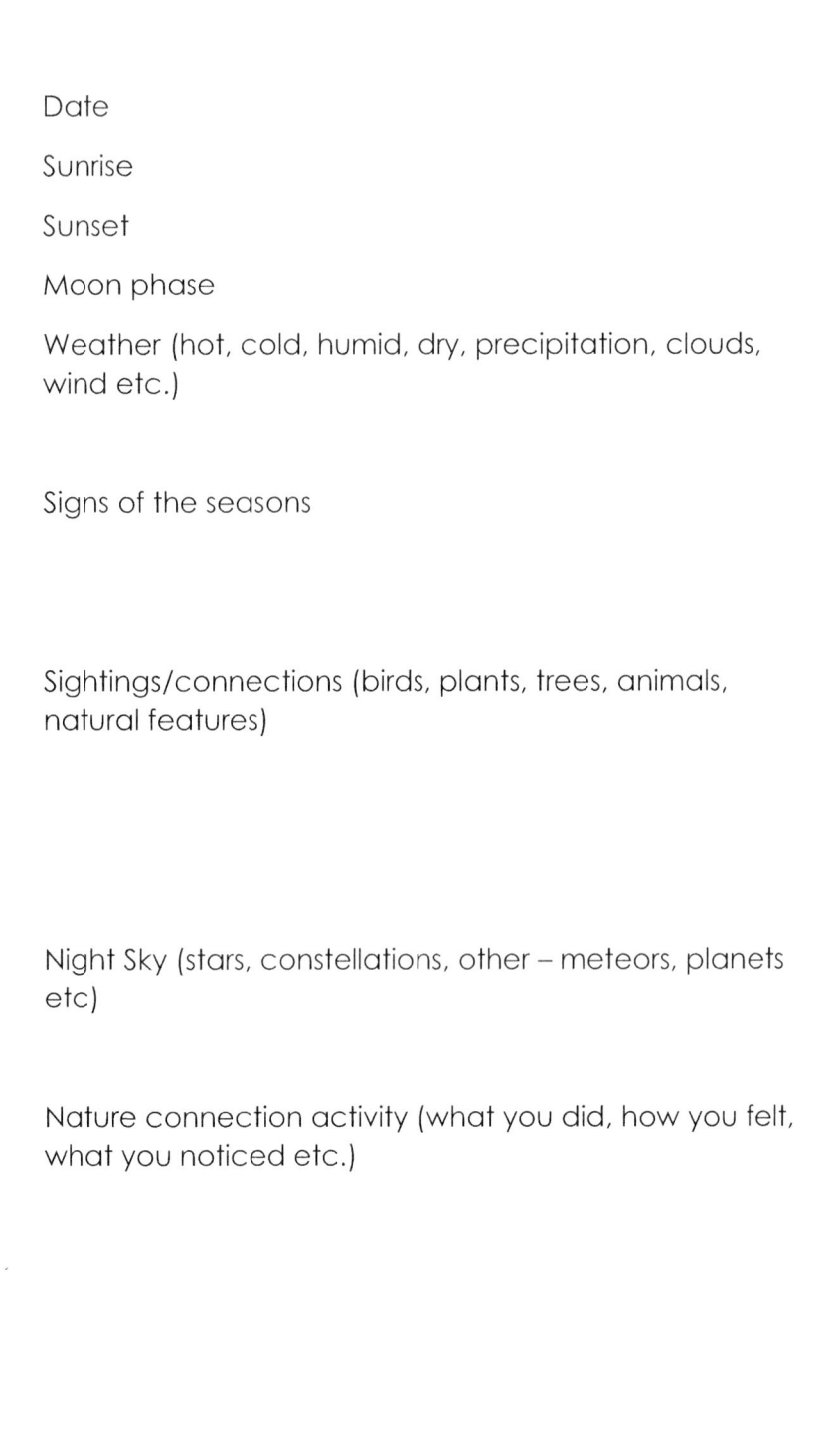

Sunrise

Sunset

Moon phase

Weather (hot, cold, humid, dry, precipitation, clouds, wind etc.)

Signs of the seasons

Sightings/connections (birds, plants, trees, animals, natural features)

Night Sky (stars, constellations, other – meteors, planets etc)

Nature connection activity (what you did, how you felt, what you noticed etc.)

Drawings, pictures, stories, poems, extra notes, gratitudes, ways I gave service to nature

Date

Sunrise

Sunset

Moon phase

Weather (hot, cold, humid, dry, precipitation, clouds, wind etc.)

Signs of the seasons

Sightings/connections (birds, plants, trees, animals, natural features)

Night Sky (stars, constellations, other – meteors, planets etc)

Nature connection activity (what you did, how you felt, what you noticed etc.)

Drawings, pictures, stories, poems, extra notes, gratitudes, ways I gave service to nature

Date

Sunrise

Sunset

Moon phase

Weather (hot, cold, humid, dry, precipitation, clouds, wind etc.)

Signs of the seasons

Sightings/connections (birds, plants, trees, animals, natural features)

Night Sky (stars, constellations, other – meteors, planets etc)

Nature connection activity (what you did, how you felt, what you noticed etc.)

Drawings, pictures, stories, poems, extra notes, gratitudes, ways I gave service to nature

Date

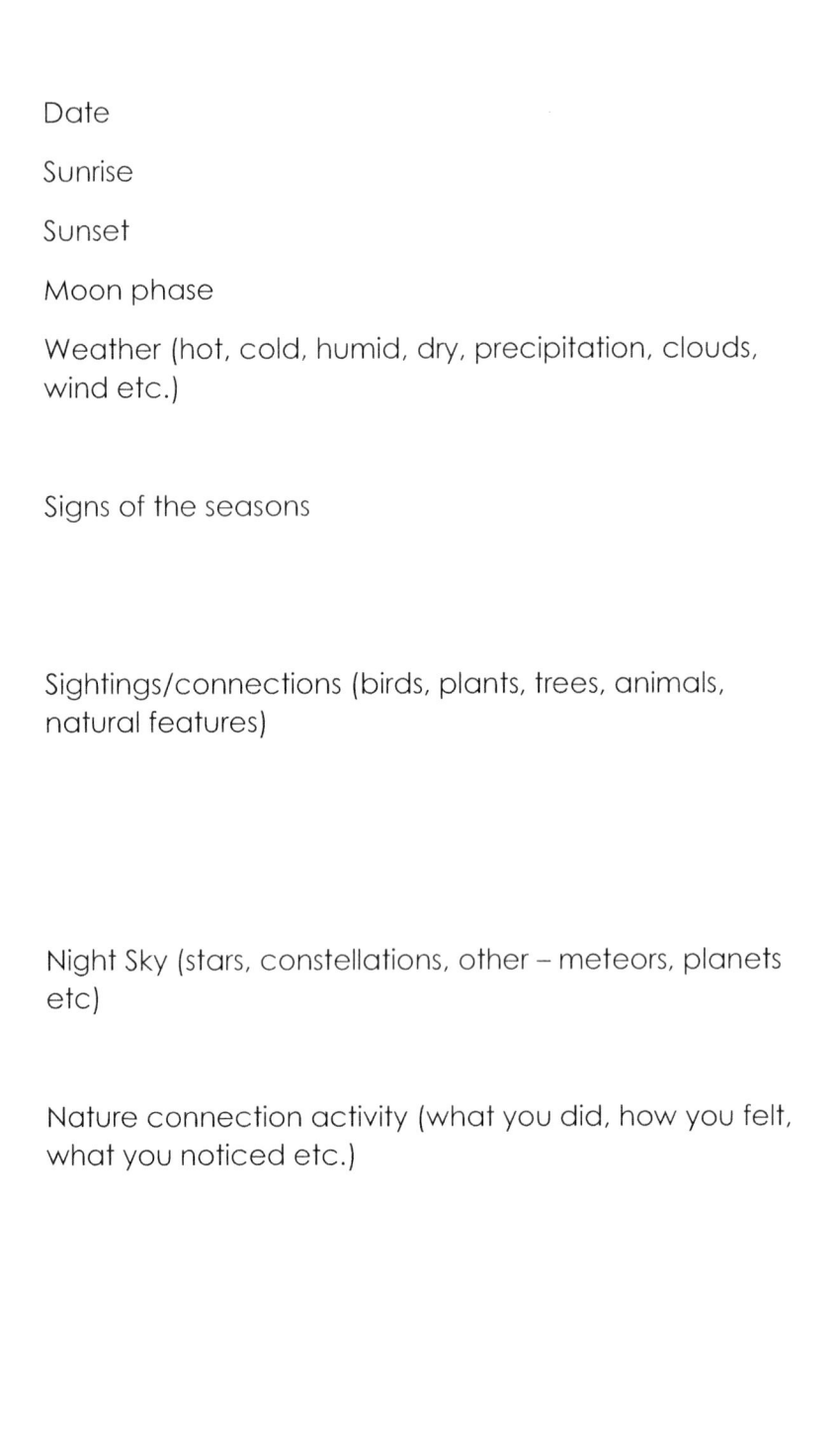

Sunrise

Sunset

Moon phase

Weather (hot, cold, humid, dry, precipitation, clouds, wind etc.)

Signs of the seasons

Sightings/connections (birds, plants, trees, animals, natural features)

Night Sky (stars, constellations, other – meteors, planets etc)

Nature connection activity (what you did, how you felt, what you noticed etc.)

Drawings, pictures, stories, poems, extra notes, gratitudes, ways I gave service to nature

Date

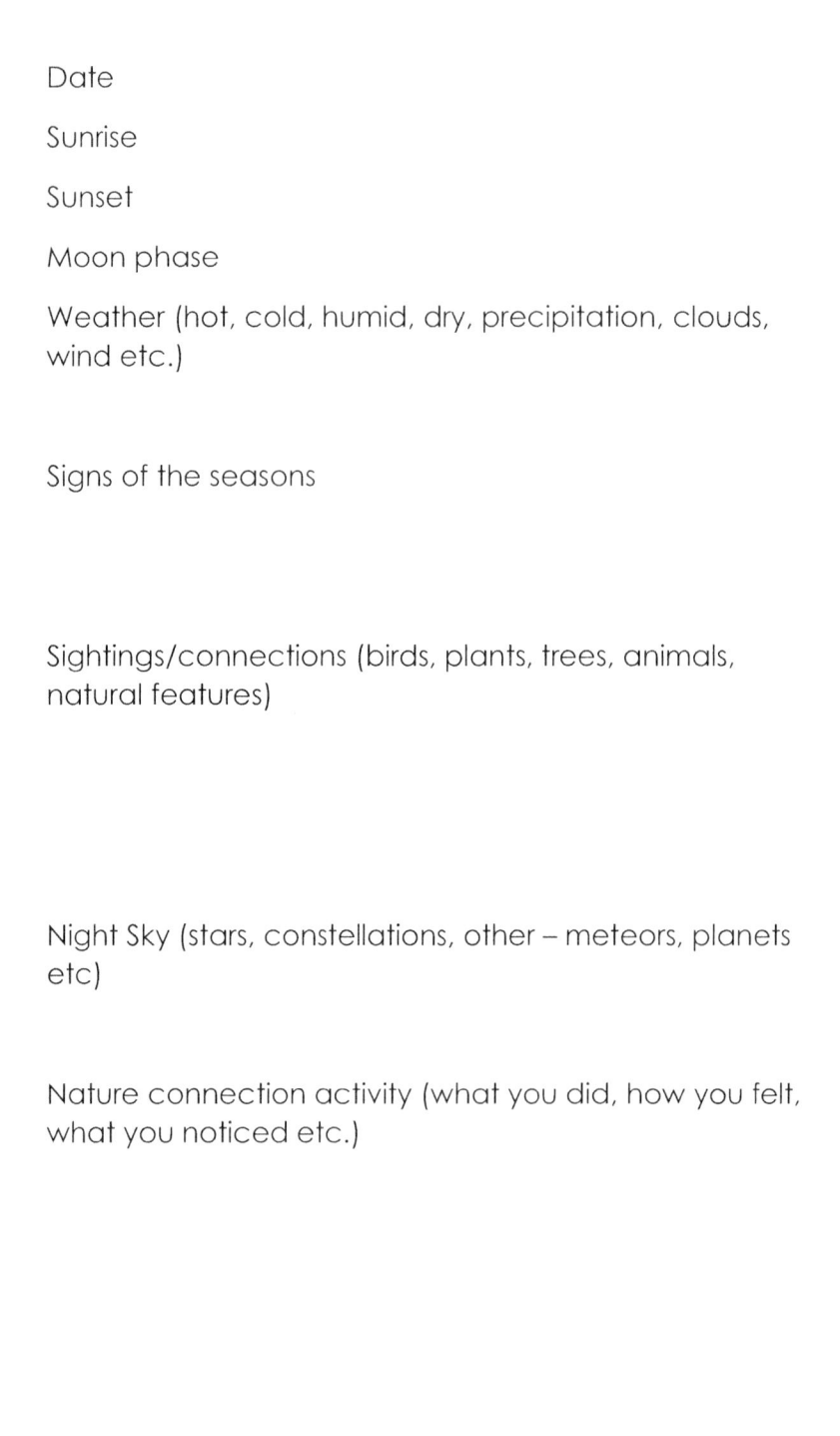

Sunrise

Sunset

Moon phase

Weather (hot, cold, humid, dry, precipitation, clouds, wind etc.)

Signs of the seasons

Sightings/connections (birds, plants, trees, animals, natural features)

Night Sky (stars, constellations, other – meteors, planets etc)

Nature connection activity (what you did, how you felt, what you noticed etc.)

Drawings, pictures, stories, poems, extra notes, gratitudes, ways I gave service to nature

Date

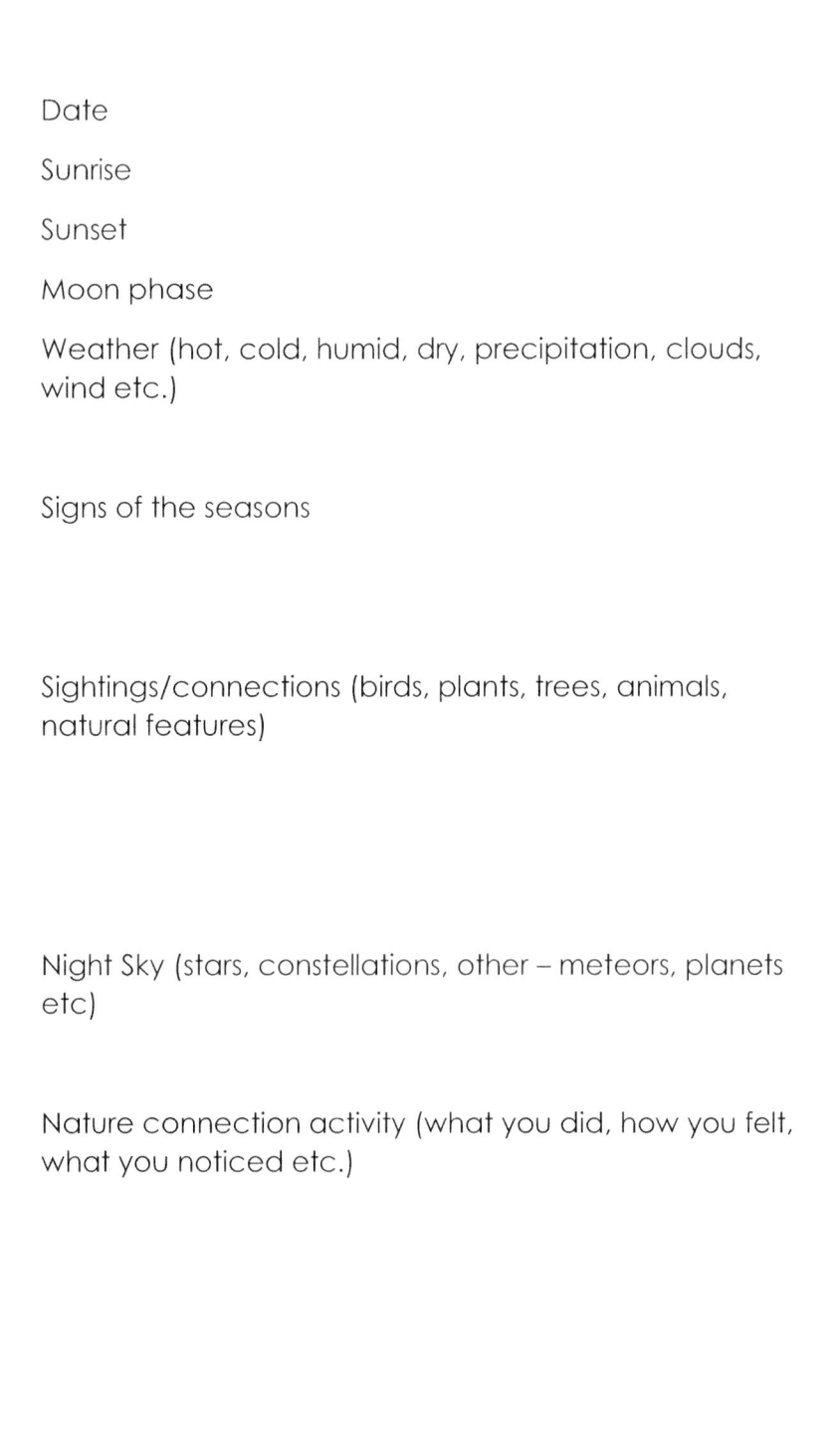

Sunrise

Sunset

Moon phase

Weather (hot, cold, humid, dry, precipitation, clouds, wind etc.)

Signs of the seasons

Sightings/connections (birds, plants, trees, animals, natural features)

Night Sky (stars, constellations, other – meteors, planets etc)

Nature connection activity (what you did, how you felt, what you noticed etc.)

Drawings, pictures, stories, poems, extra notes, gratitudes, ways I gave service to nature

Date

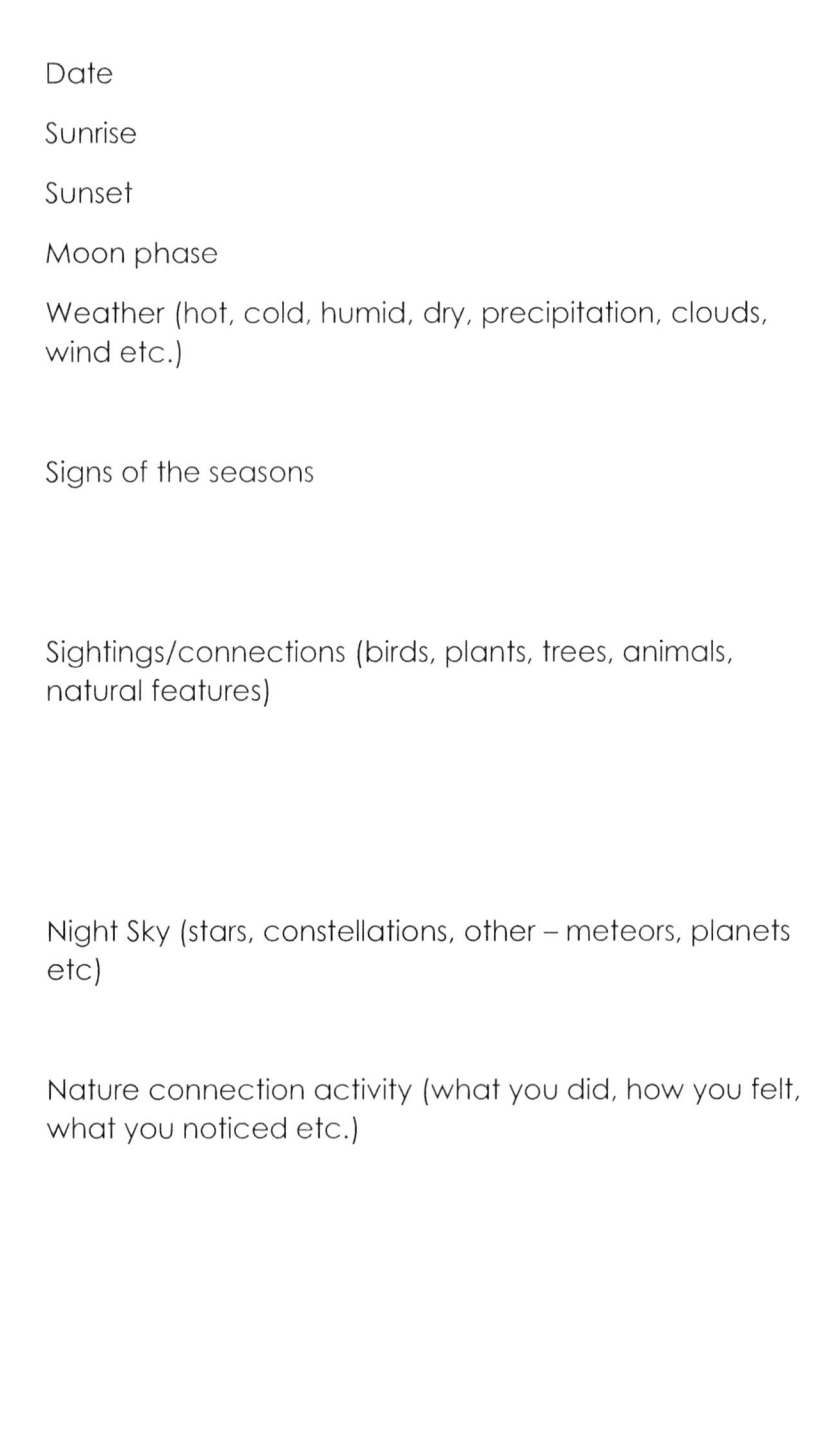

Sunrise

Sunset

Moon phase

Weather (hot, cold, humid, dry, precipitation, clouds, wind etc.)

Signs of the seasons

Sightings/connections (birds, plants, trees, animals, natural features)

Night Sky (stars, constellations, other – meteors, planets etc)

Nature connection activity (what you did, how you felt, what you noticed etc.)

Drawings, pictures, stories, poems, extra notes, gratitudes, ways I gave service to nature

Date

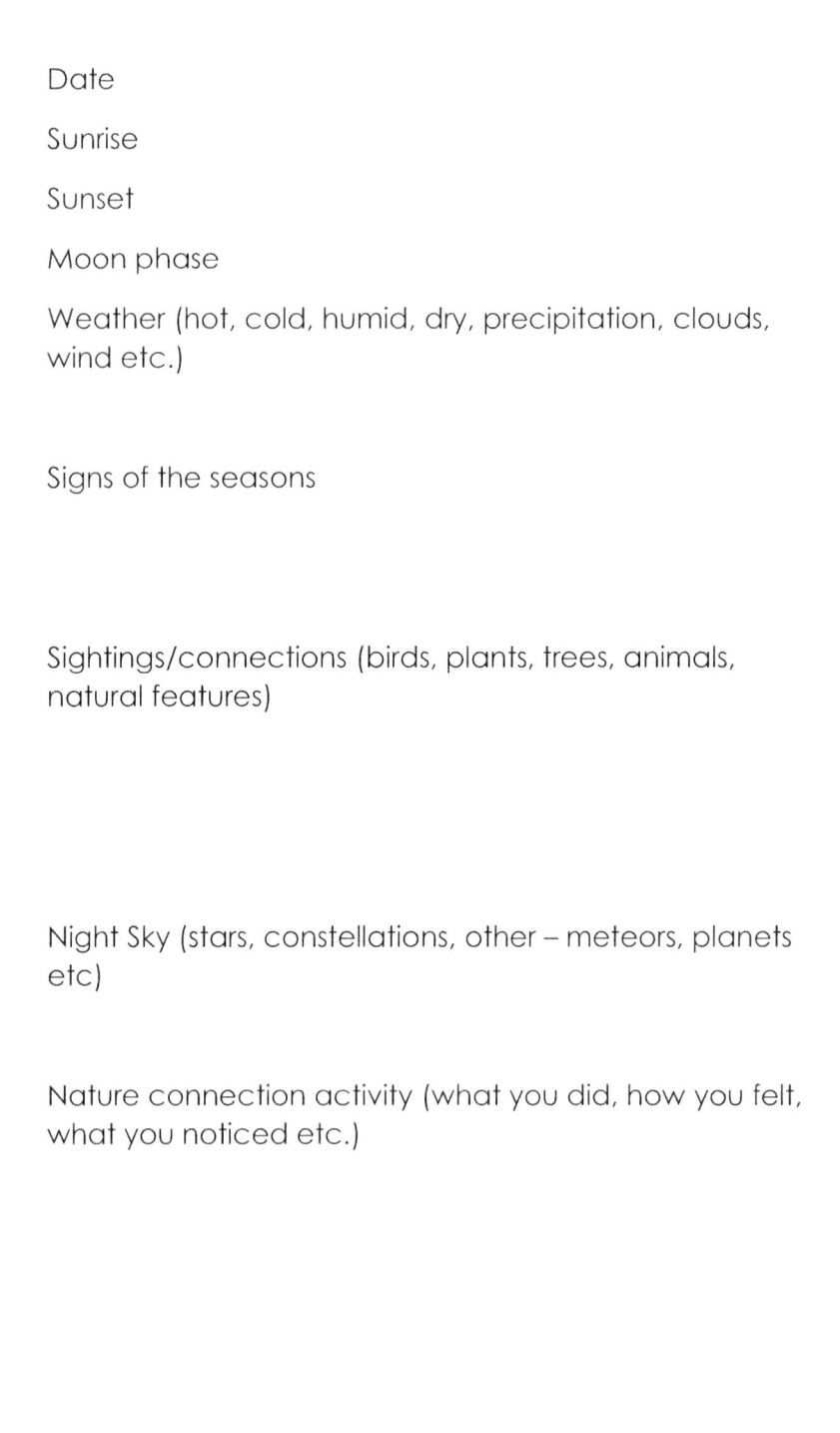

Sunrise

Sunset

Moon phase

Weather (hot, cold, humid, dry, precipitation, clouds, wind etc.)

Signs of the seasons

Sightings/connections (birds, plants, trees, animals, natural features)

Night Sky (stars, constellations, other – meteors, planets etc)

Nature connection activity (what you did, how you felt, what you noticed etc.)

Drawings, pictures, stories, poems, extra notes, gratitudes, ways I gave service to nature

Date

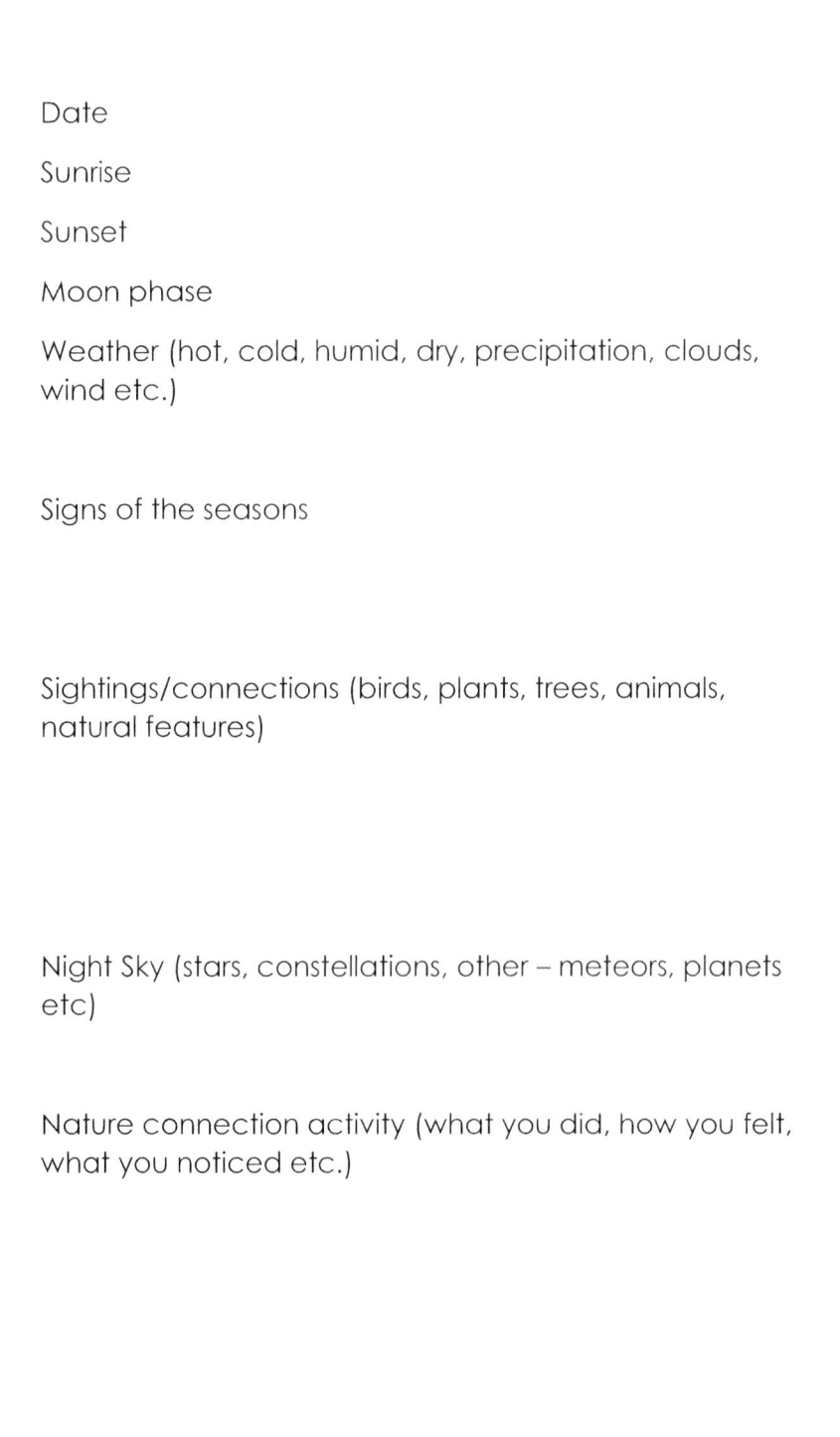

Sunrise

Sunset

Moon phase

Weather (hot, cold, humid, dry, precipitation, clouds, wind etc.)

Signs of the seasons

Sightings/connections (birds, plants, trees, animals, natural features)

Night Sky (stars, constellations, other – meteors, planets etc)

Nature connection activity (what you did, how you felt, what you noticed etc.)

Drawings, pictures, stories, poems, extra notes, gratitudes, ways I gave service to nature

Date

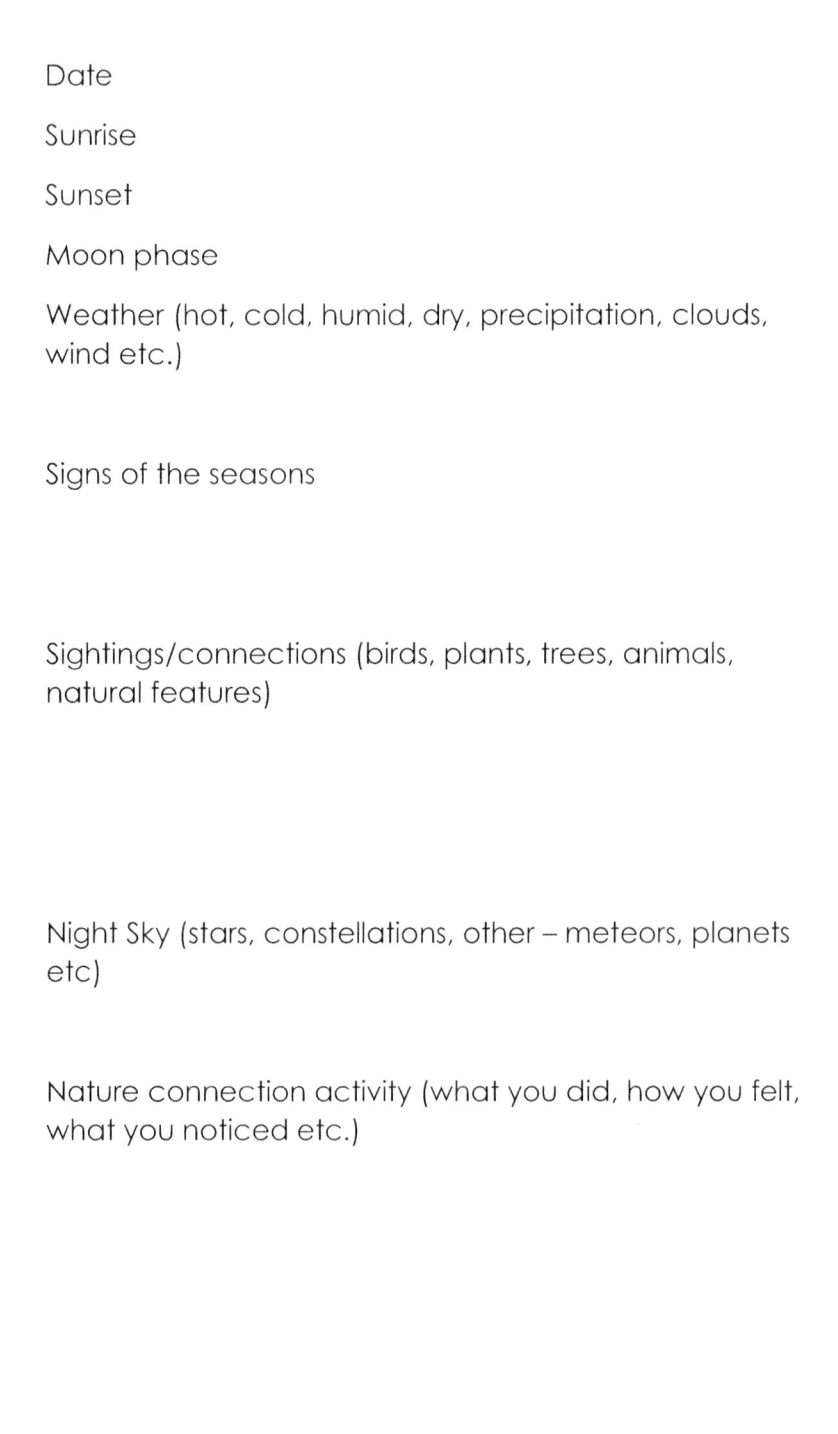

Sunrise

Sunset

Moon phase

Weather (hot, cold, humid, dry, precipitation, clouds, wind etc.)

Signs of the seasons

Sightings/connections (birds, plants, trees, animals, natural features)

Night Sky (stars, constellations, other – meteors, planets etc)

Nature connection activity (what you did, how you felt, what you noticed etc.)

Drawings, pictures, stories, poems, extra notes, gratitudes, ways I gave service to nature

Date

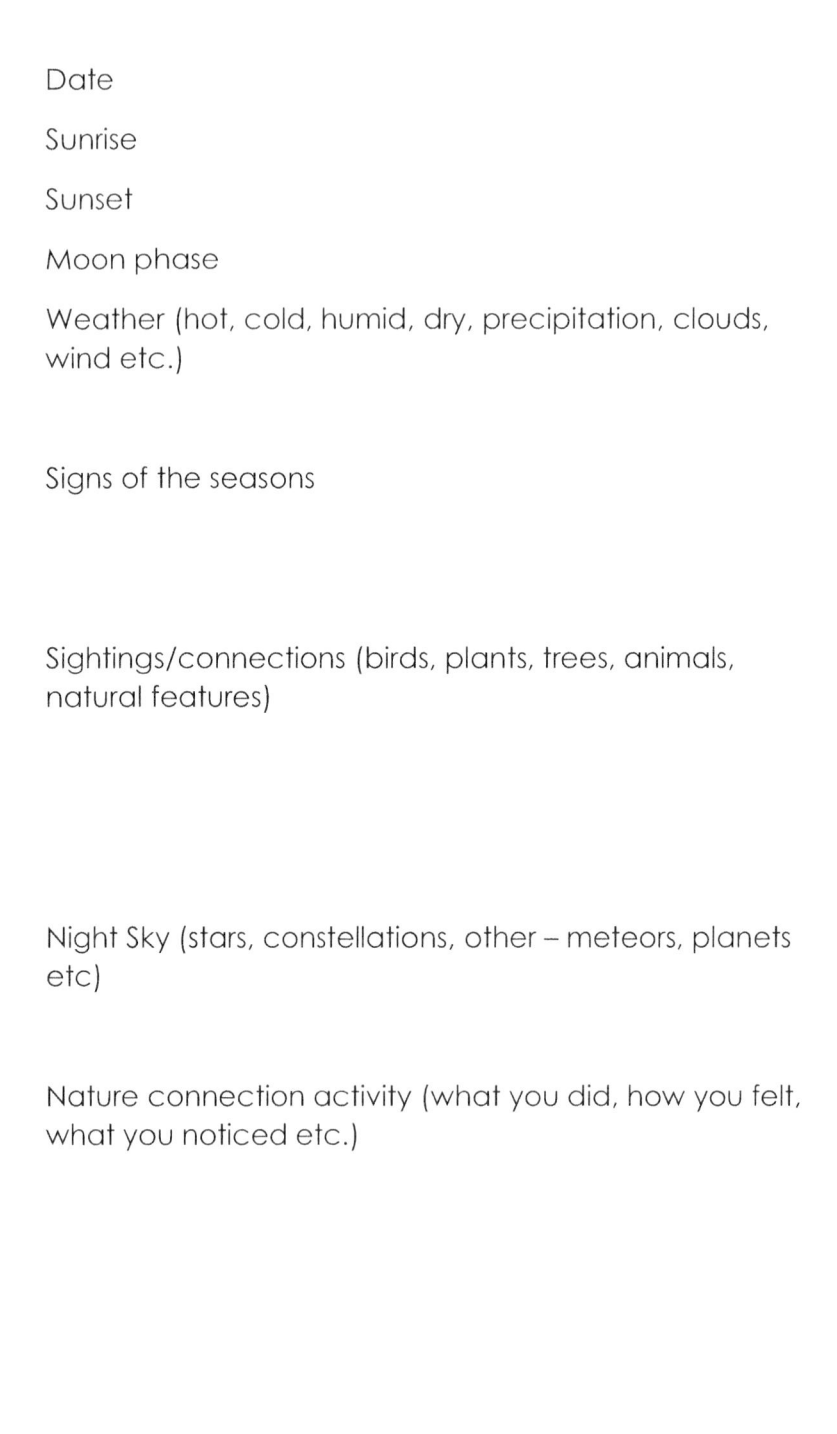

Sunrise

Sunset

Moon phase

Weather (hot, cold, humid, dry, precipitation, clouds, wind etc.)

Signs of the seasons

Sightings/connections (birds, plants, trees, animals, natural features)

Night Sky (stars, constellations, other – meteors, planets etc)

Nature connection activity (what you did, how you felt, what you noticed etc.)

Drawings, pictures, stories, poems, extra notes, gratitudes, ways I gave service to nature

Date

Sunrise

Sunset

Moon phase

Weather (hot, cold, humid, dry, precipitation, clouds, wind etc.)

Signs of the seasons

Sightings/connections (birds, plants, trees, animals, natural features)

Night Sky (stars, constellations, other – meteors, planets etc)

Nature connection activity (what you did, how you felt, what you noticed etc.)

Drawings, pictures, stories, poems, extra notes, gratitudes, ways I gave service to nature

Date

Sunrise

Sunset

Moon phase

Weather (hot, cold, humid, dry, precipitation, clouds, wind etc.)

Signs of the seasons

Sightings/connections (birds, plants, trees, animals, natural features)

Night Sky (stars, constellations, other – meteors, planets etc)

Nature connection activity (what you did, how you felt, what you noticed etc.)

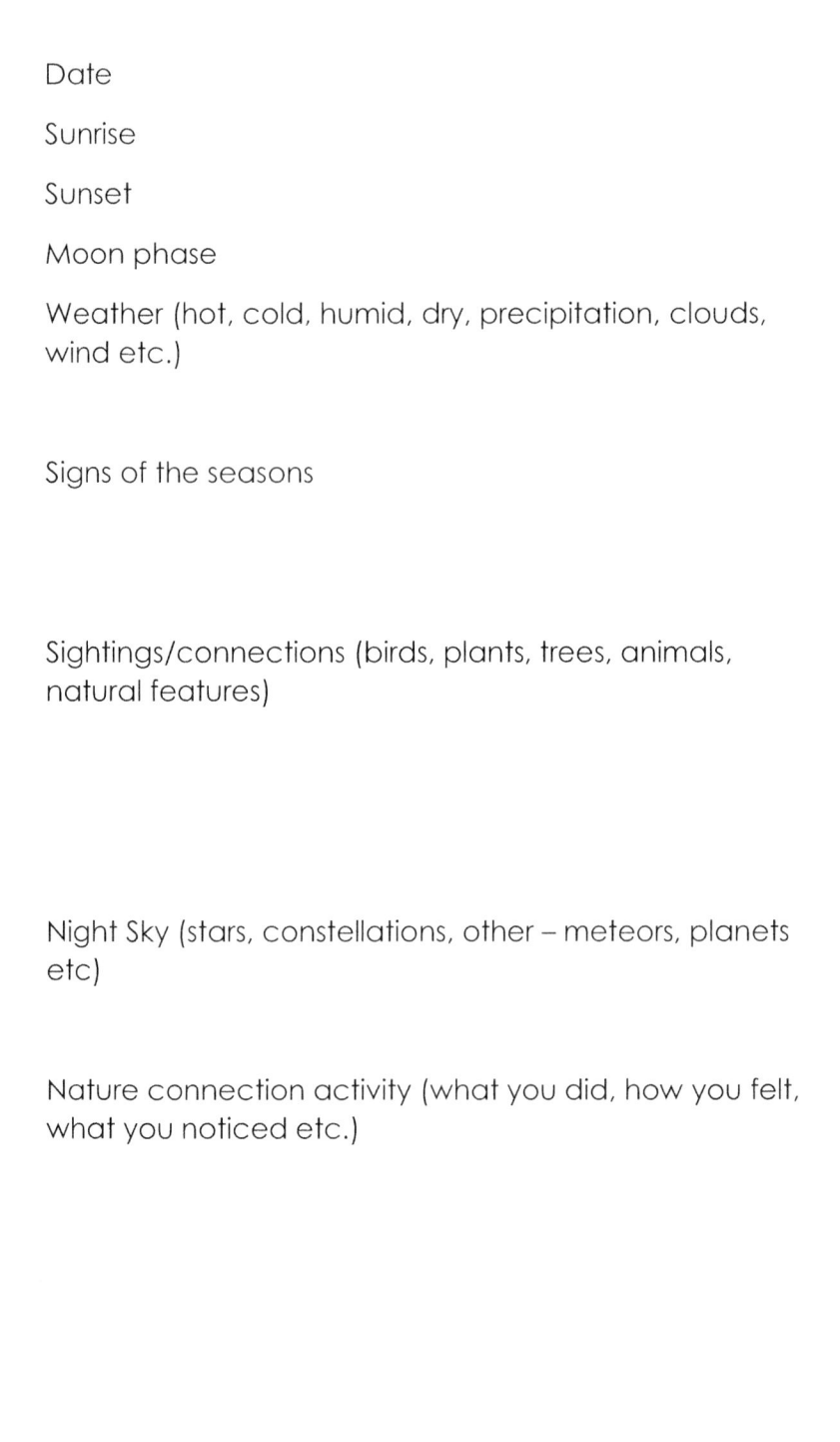

Drawings, pictures, stories, poems, extra notes, gratitudes, ways I gave service to nature

Date

Sunrise

Sunset

Moon phase

Weather (hot, cold, humid, dry, precipitation, clouds, wind etc.)

Signs of the seasons

Sightings/connections (birds, plants, trees, animals, natural features)

Night Sky (stars, constellations, other – meteors, planets etc)

Nature connection activity (what you did, how you felt, what you noticed etc.)

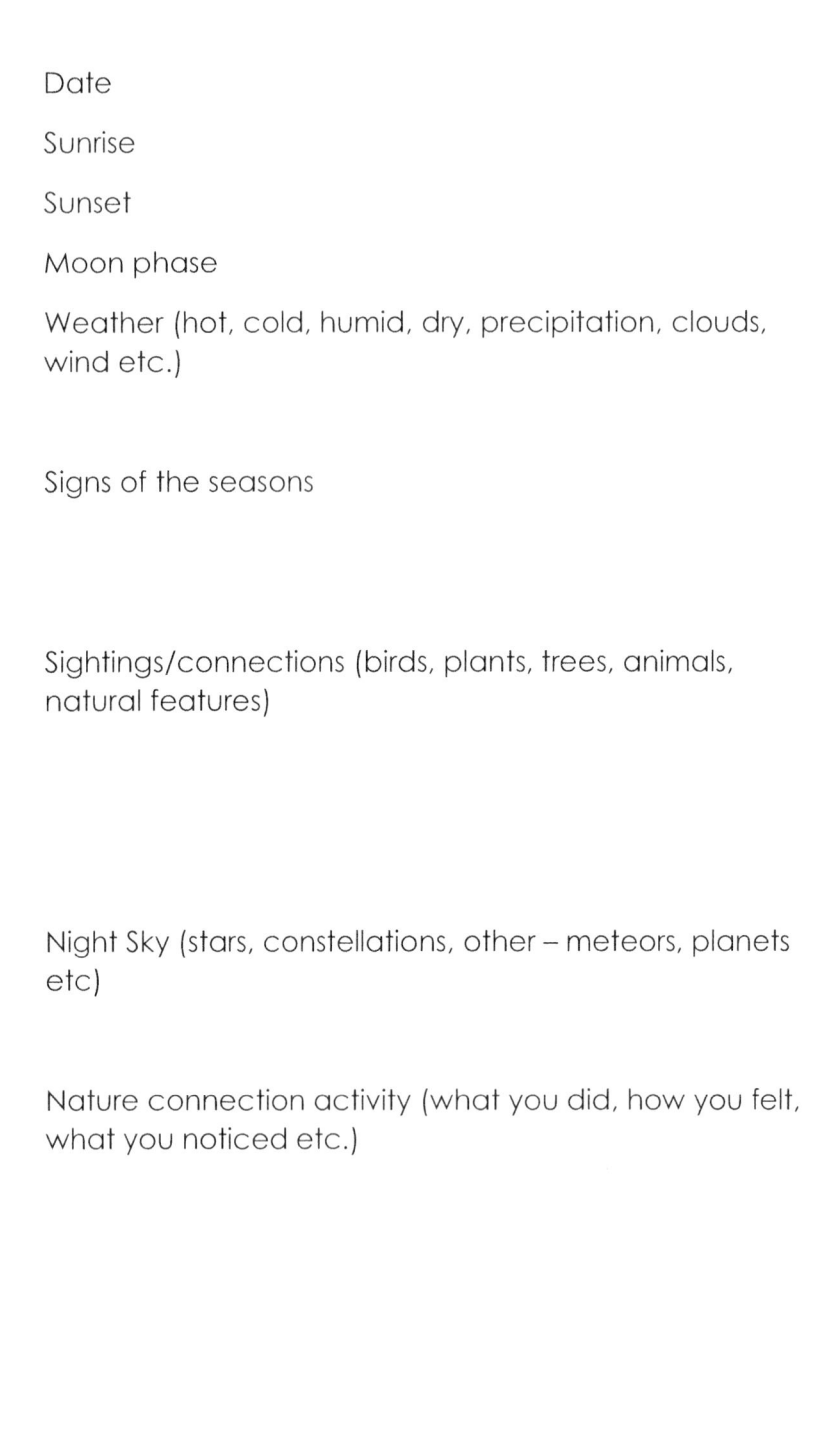

Drawings, pictures, stories, poems, extra notes, gratitudes, ways I gave service to nature

Date

Sunrise

Sunset

Moon phase

Weather (hot, cold, humid, dry, precipitation, clouds, wind etc.)

Signs of the seasons

Sightings/connections (birds, plants, trees, animals, natural features)

Night Sky (stars, constellations, other – meteors, planets etc)

Nature connection activity (what you did, how you felt, what you noticed etc.)

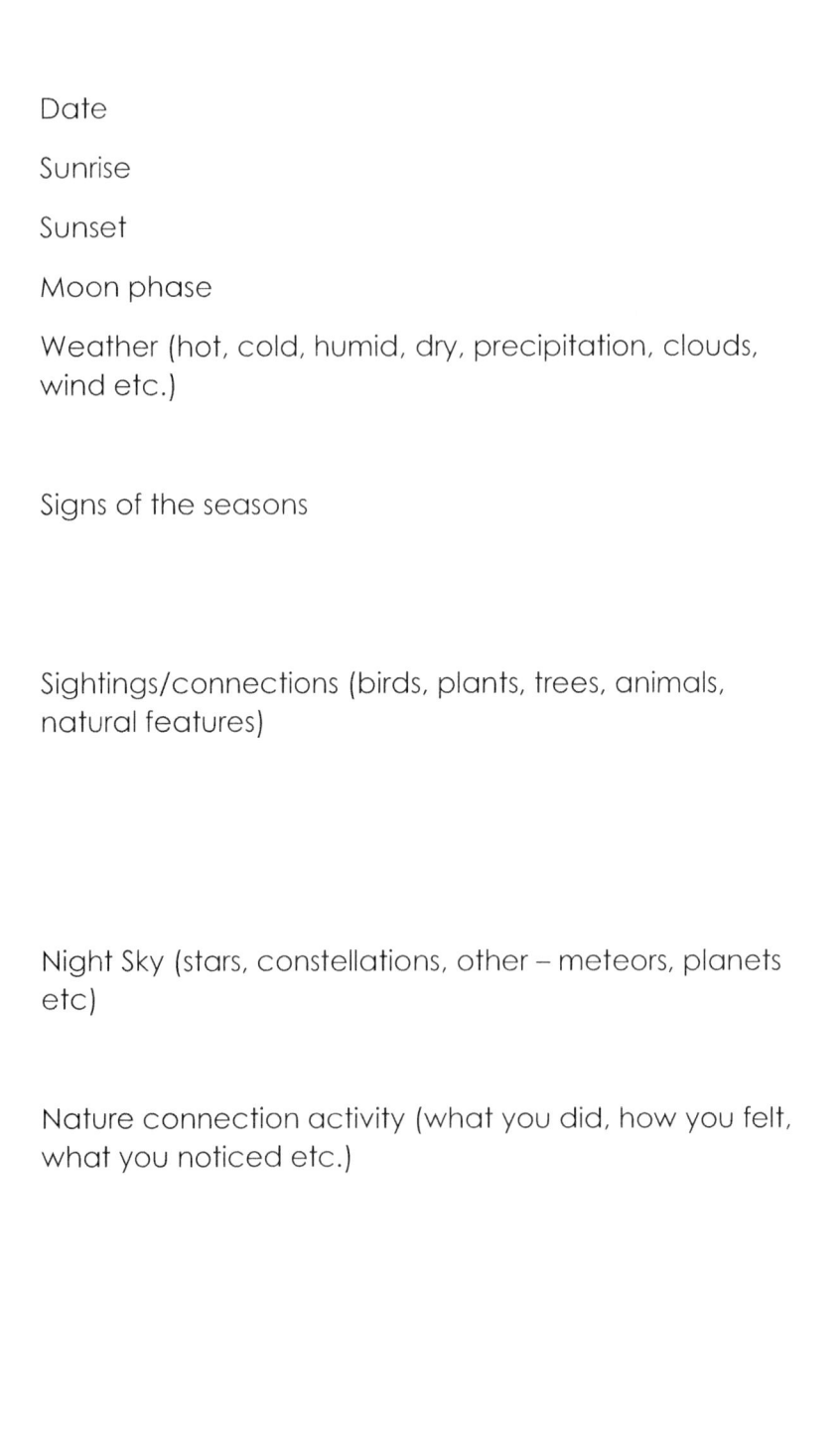

Drawings, pictures, stories, poems, extra notes, gratitudes, ways I gave service to nature

Date

Sunrise

Sunset

Moon phase

Weather (hot, cold, humid, dry, precipitation, clouds, wind etc.)

Signs of the seasons

Sightings/connections (birds, plants, trees, animals, natural features)

Night Sky (stars, constellations, other – meteors, planets etc)

Nature connection activity (what you did, how you felt, what you noticed etc.)

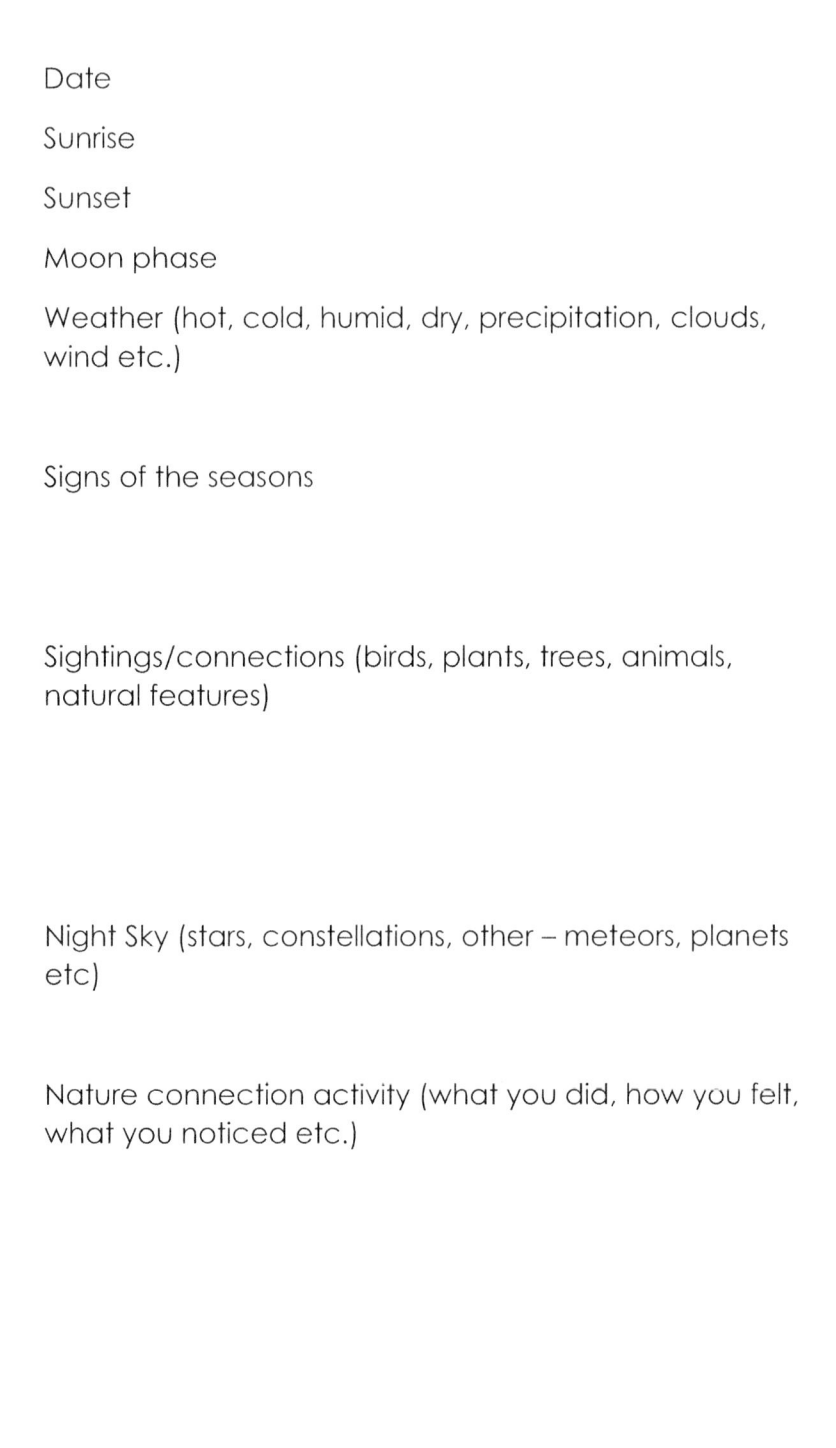

Drawings, pictures, stories, poems, extra notes, gratitudes, ways I gave service to nature

Date

Sunrise

Sunset

Moon phase

Weather (hot, cold, humid, dry, precipitation, clouds, wind etc.)

Signs of the seasons

Sightings/connections (birds, plants, trees, animals, natural features)

Night Sky (stars, constellations, other – meteors, planets etc)

Nature connection activity (what you did, how you felt, what you noticed etc.)

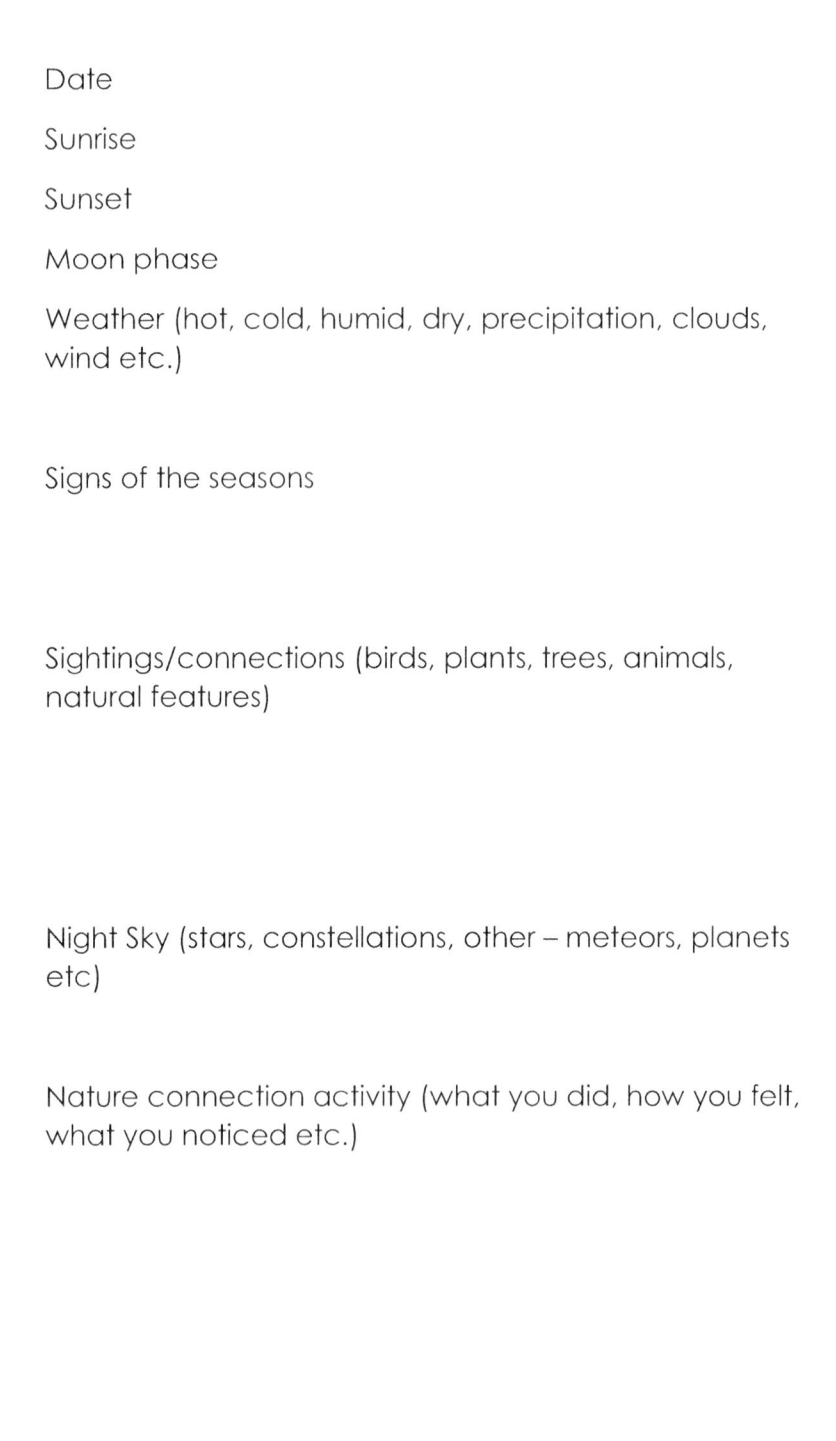

Drawings, pictures, stories, poems, extra notes, gratitudes, ways I gave service to nature

Date

Sunrise

Sunset

Moon phase

Weather (hot, cold, humid, dry, precipitation, clouds, wind etc.)

Signs of the seasons

Sightings/connections (birds, plants, trees, animals, natural features)

Night Sky (stars, constellations, other – meteors, planets etc)

Nature connection activity (what you did, how you felt, what you noticed etc.)

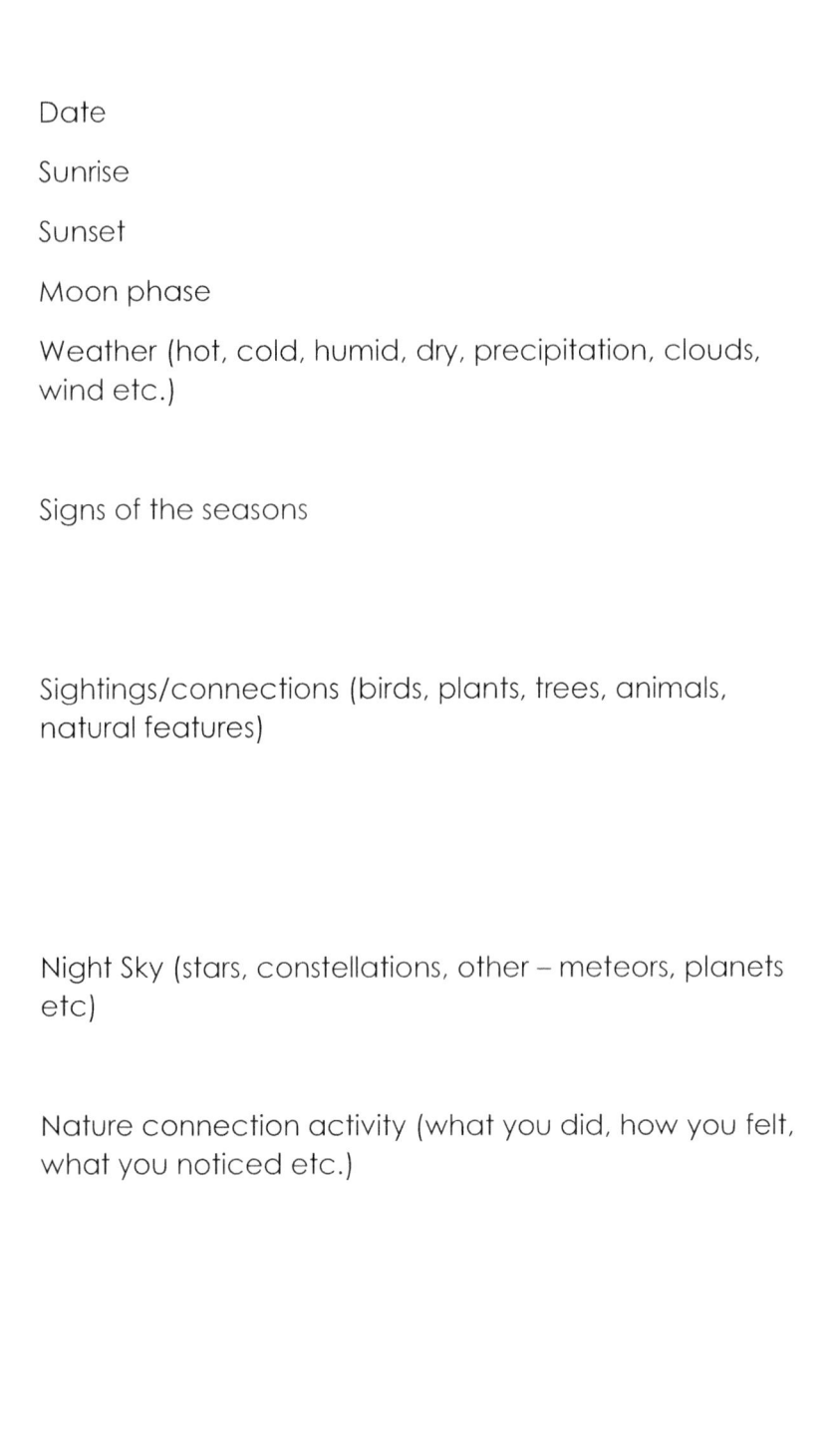

Drawings, pictures, stories, poems, extra notes, gratitudes, ways I gave service to nature

Date

Sunrise

Sunset

Moon phase

Weather (hot, cold, humid, dry, precipitation, clouds, wind etc.)

Signs of the seasons

Sightings/connections (birds, plants, trees, animals, natural features)

Night Sky (stars, constellations, other – meteors, planets etc)

Nature connection activity (what you did, how you felt, what you noticed etc.)

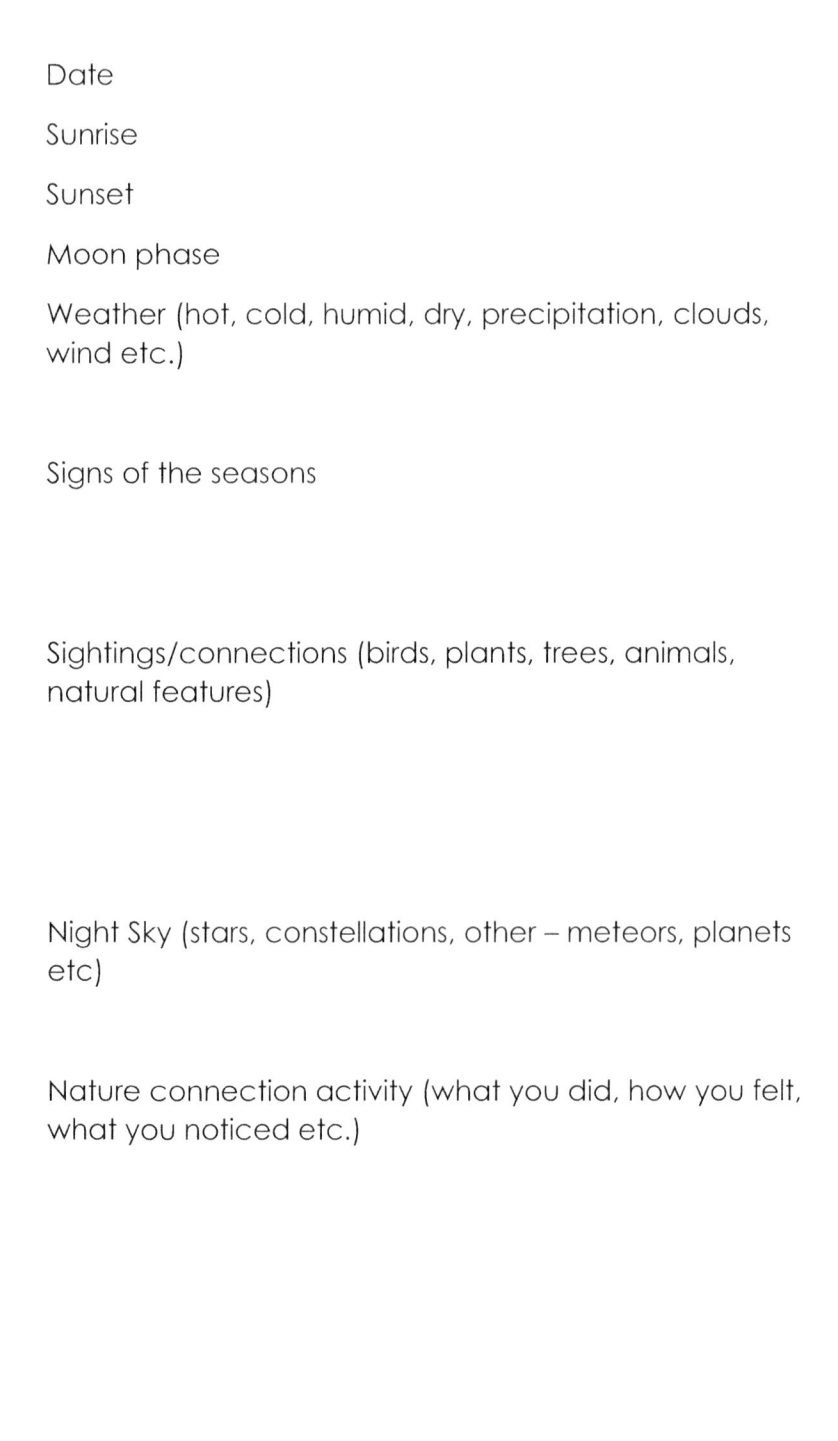

Drawings, pictures, stories, poems, extra notes, gratitudes, ways I gave service to nature

- Date

Sunrise

Sunset

Moon phase

Weather (hot, cold, humid, dry, precipitation, clouds, wind etc.)

Signs of the seasons

Sightings/connections (birds, plants, trees, animals, natural features)

Night Sky (stars, constellations, other – meteors, planets etc)

Nature connection activity (what you did, how you felt, what you noticed etc.)

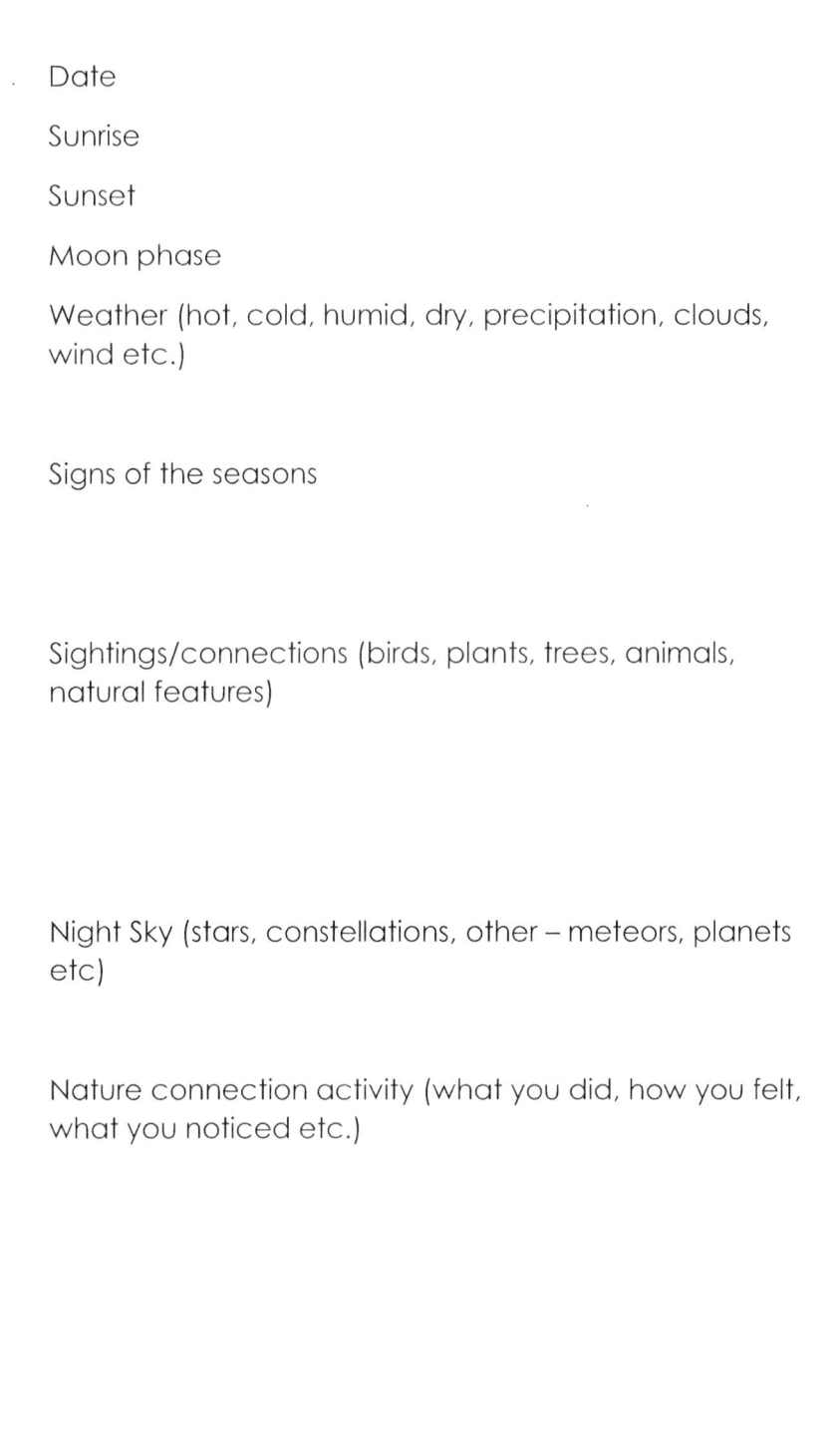

Drawings, pictures, stories, poems, extra notes, gratitudes, ways I gave service to nature

Date

Sunrise

Sunset

Moon phase

Weather (hot, cold, humid, dry, precipitation, clouds, wind etc.)

Signs of the seasons

Sightings/connections (birds, plants, trees, animals, natural features)

Night Sky (stars, constellations, other – meteors, planets etc)

Nature connection activity (what you did, how you felt, what you noticed etc.)

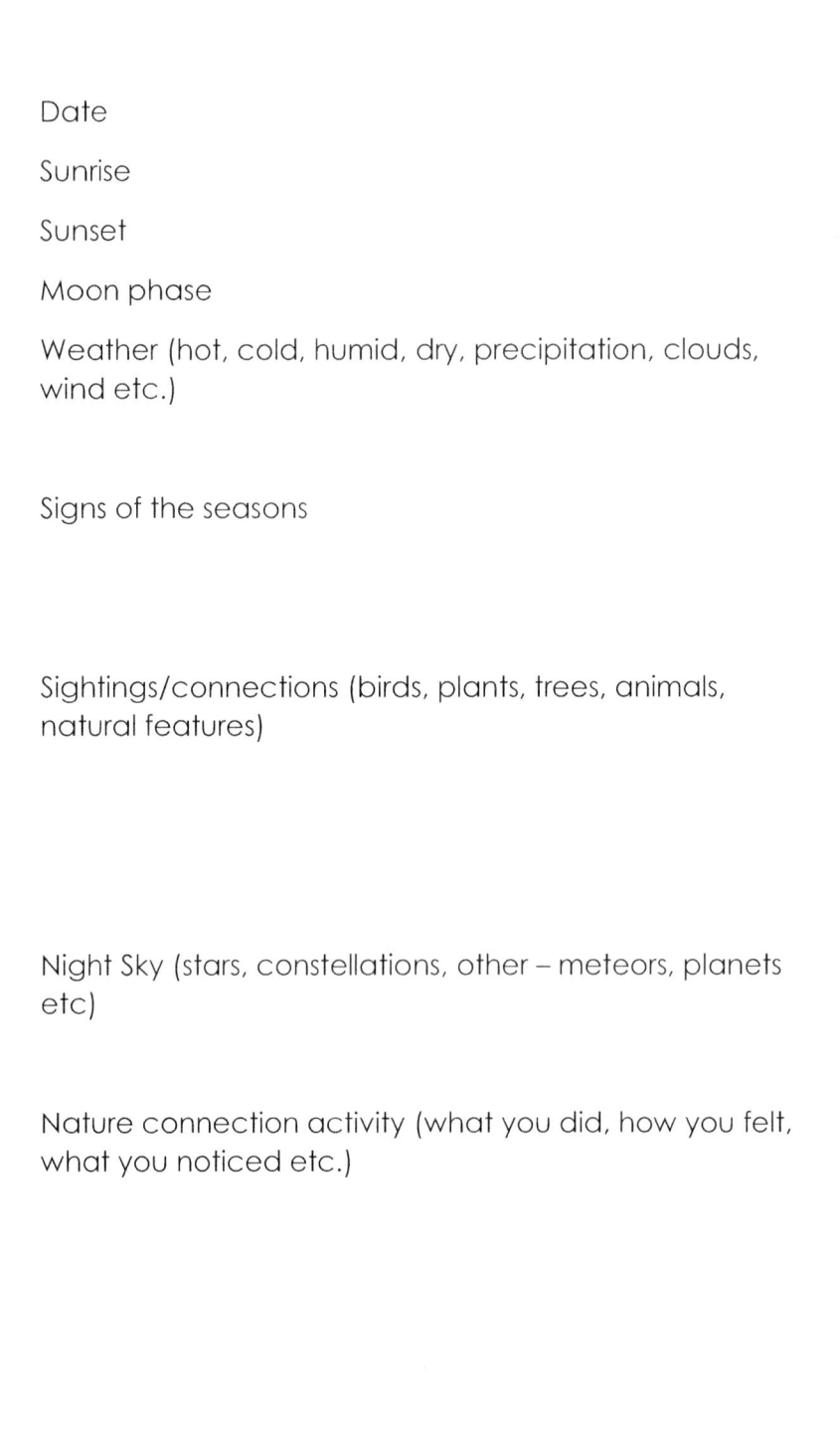

Drawings, pictures, stories, poems, extra notes, gratitudes, ways I gave service to nature

Date

Sunrise

Sunset

Moon phase

Weather (hot, cold, humid, dry, precipitation, clouds, wind etc.)

Signs of the seasons

Sightings/connections (birds, plants, trees, animals, natural features)

Night Sky (stars, constellations, other – meteors, planets etc)

Nature connection activity (what you did, how you felt, what you noticed etc.)

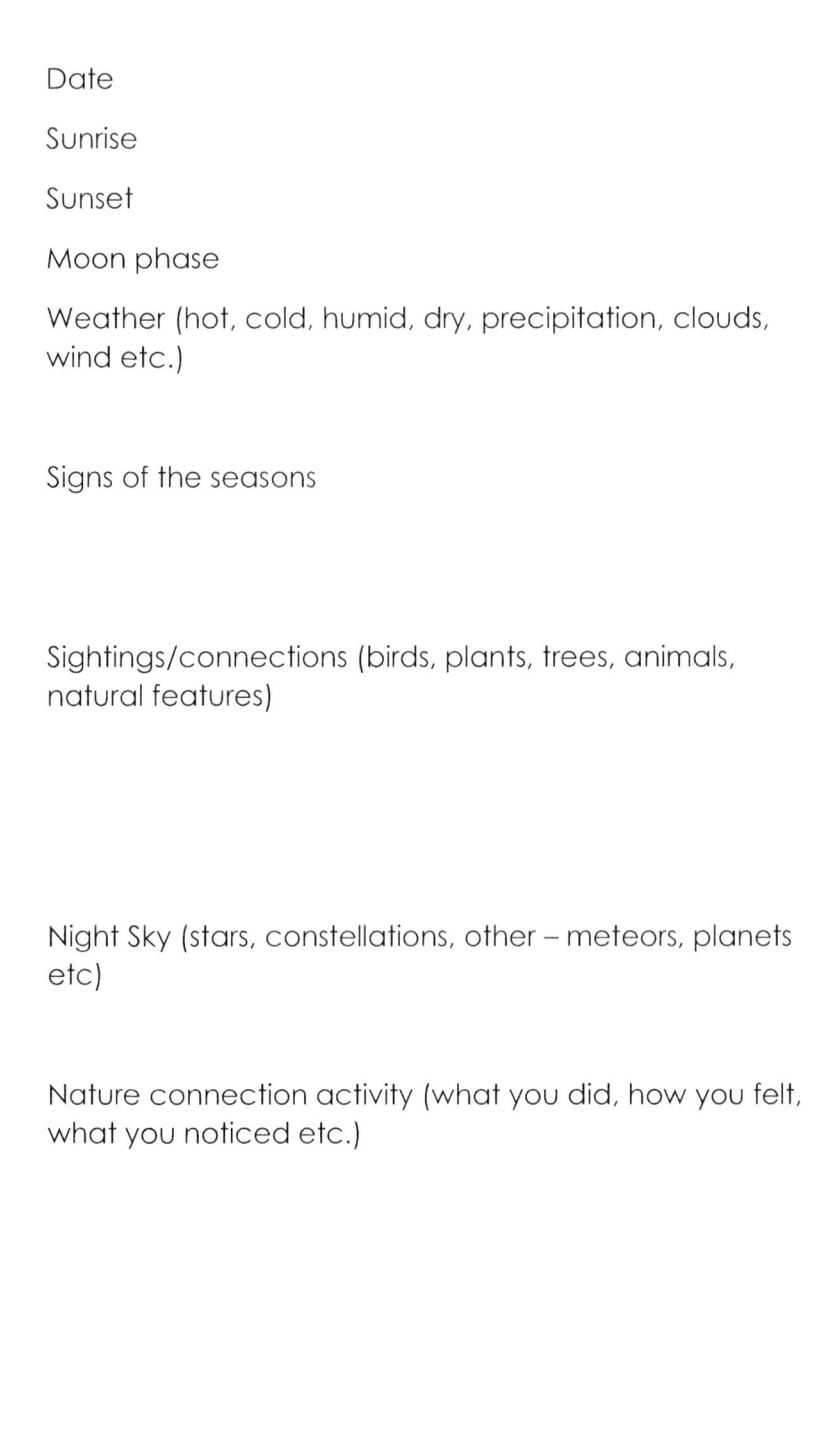

Drawings, pictures, stories, poems, extra notes, gratitudes, ways I gave service to nature

Date

Sunrise

Sunset

Moon phase

Weather (hot, cold, humid, dry, precipitation, clouds, wind etc.)

Signs of the seasons

Sightings/connections (birds, plants, trees, animals, natural features)

Night Sky (stars, constellations, other – meteors, planets etc)

Nature connection activity (what you did, how you felt, what you noticed etc.)

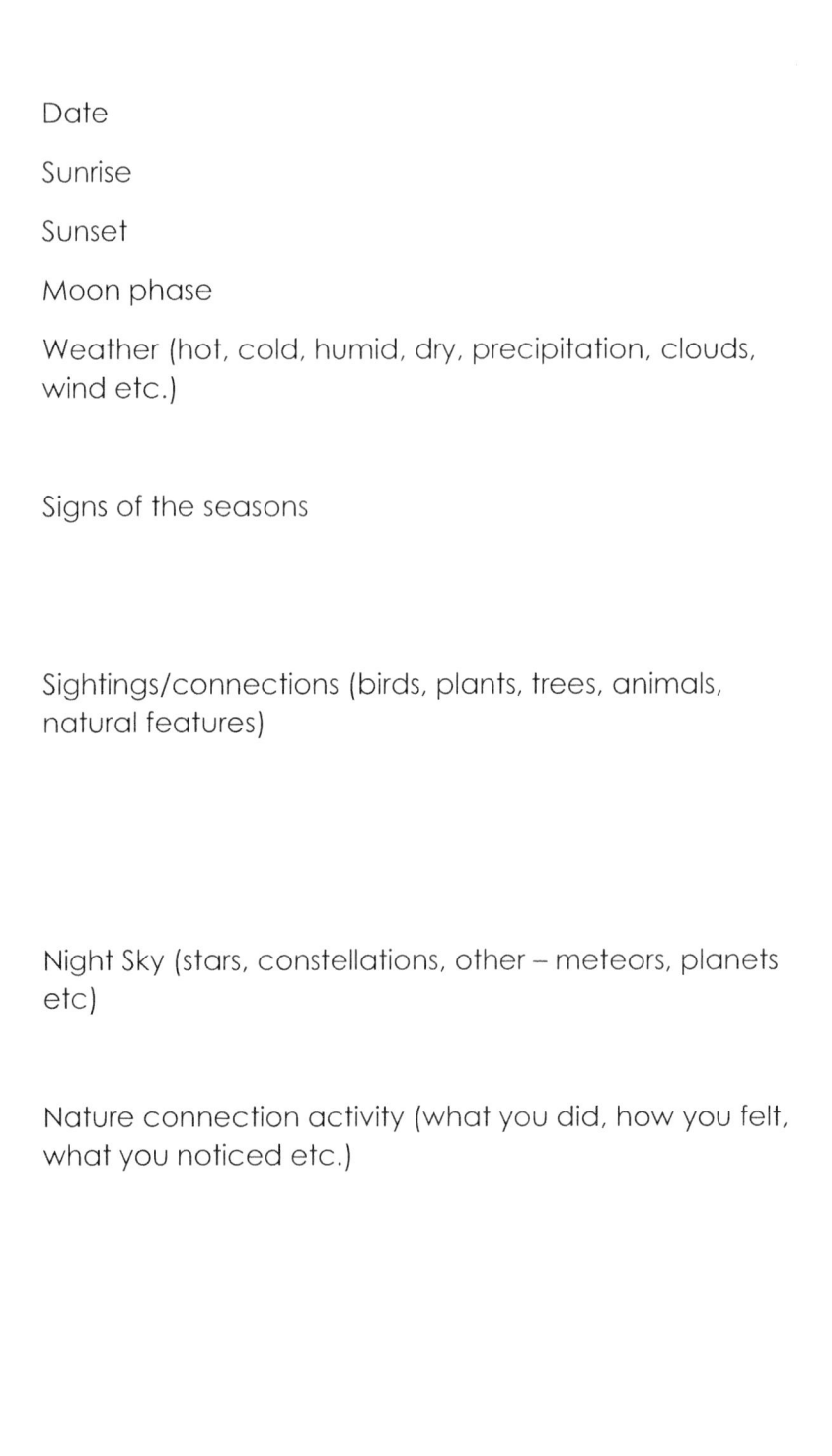

Drawings, pictures, stories, poems, extra notes, gratitudes, ways I gave service to nature

Date

Sunrise

Sunset

Moon phase

Weather (hot, cold, humid, dry, precipitation, clouds, wind etc.)

Signs of the seasons

Sightings/connections (birds, plants, trees, animals, natural features)

Night Sky (stars, constellations, other – meteors, planets etc)

Nature connection activity (what you did, how you felt, what you noticed etc.)

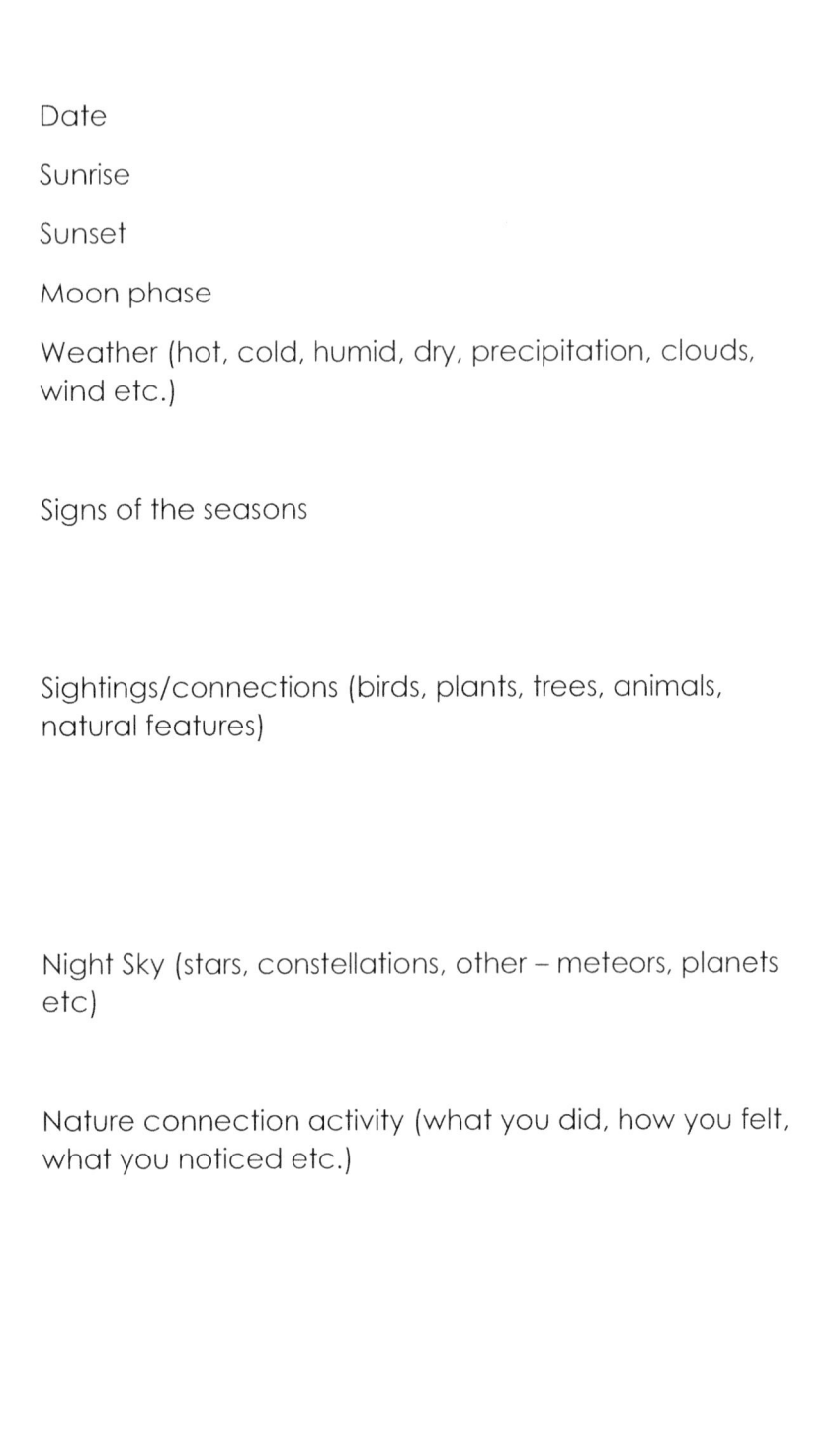

Drawings, pictures, stories, poems, extra notes, gratitudes, ways I gave service to nature

Date

Sunrise

Sunset

Moon phase

Weather (hot, cold, humid, dry, precipitation, clouds, wind etc.)

Signs of the seasons

Sightings/connections (birds, plants, trees, animals, natural features)

Night Sky (stars, constellations, other – meteors, planets etc)

Nature connection activity (what you did, how you felt, what you noticed etc.)

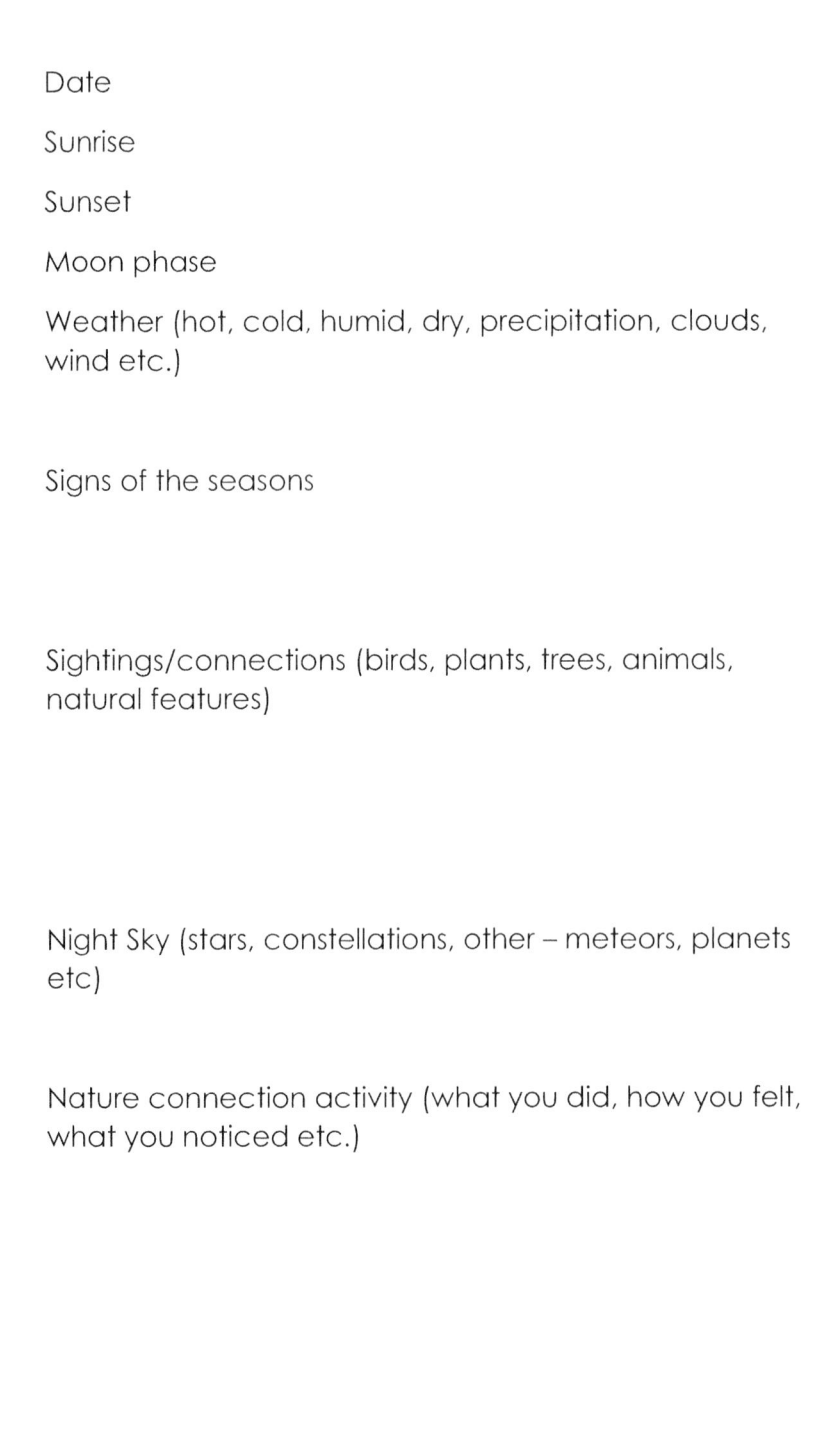

Drawings, pictures, stories, poems, extra notes, gratitudes, ways I gave service to nature

Date

Sunrise

Sunset

Moon phase

Weather (hot, cold, humid, dry, precipitation, clouds, wind etc.)

Signs of the seasons

Sightings/connections (birds, plants, trees, animals, natural features)

Night Sky (stars, constellations, other – meteors, planets etc)

Nature connection activity (what you did, how you felt, what you noticed etc.)

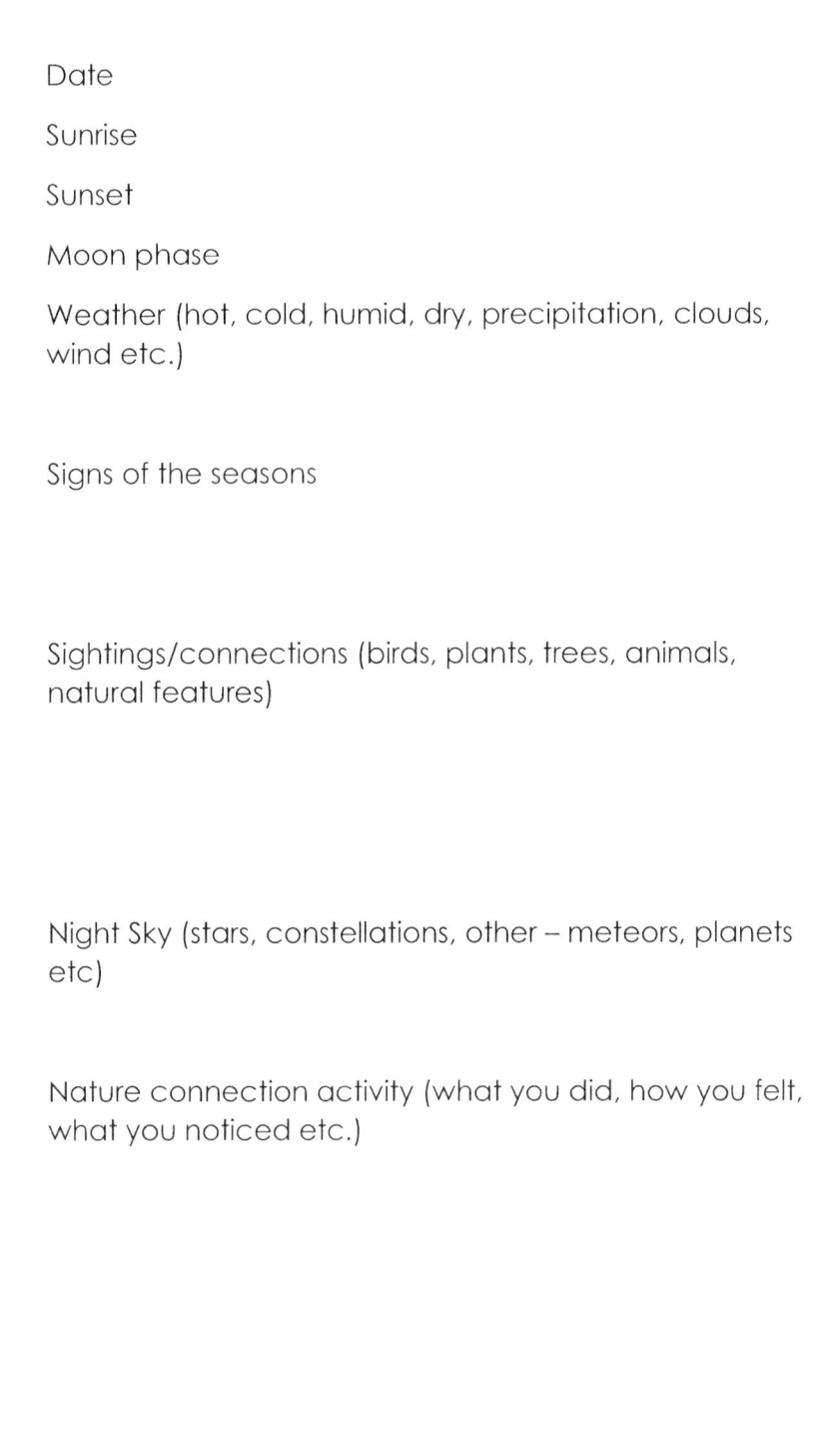

Drawings, pictures, stories, poems, extra notes, gratitudes, ways I gave service to nature

Date

Sunrise

Sunset

Moon phase

Weather (hot, cold, humid, dry, precipitation, clouds, wind etc.)

Signs of the seasons

Sightings/connections (birds, plants, trees, animals, natural features)

Night Sky (stars, constellations, other – meteors, planets etc)

Nature connection activity (what you did, how you felt, what you noticed etc.)

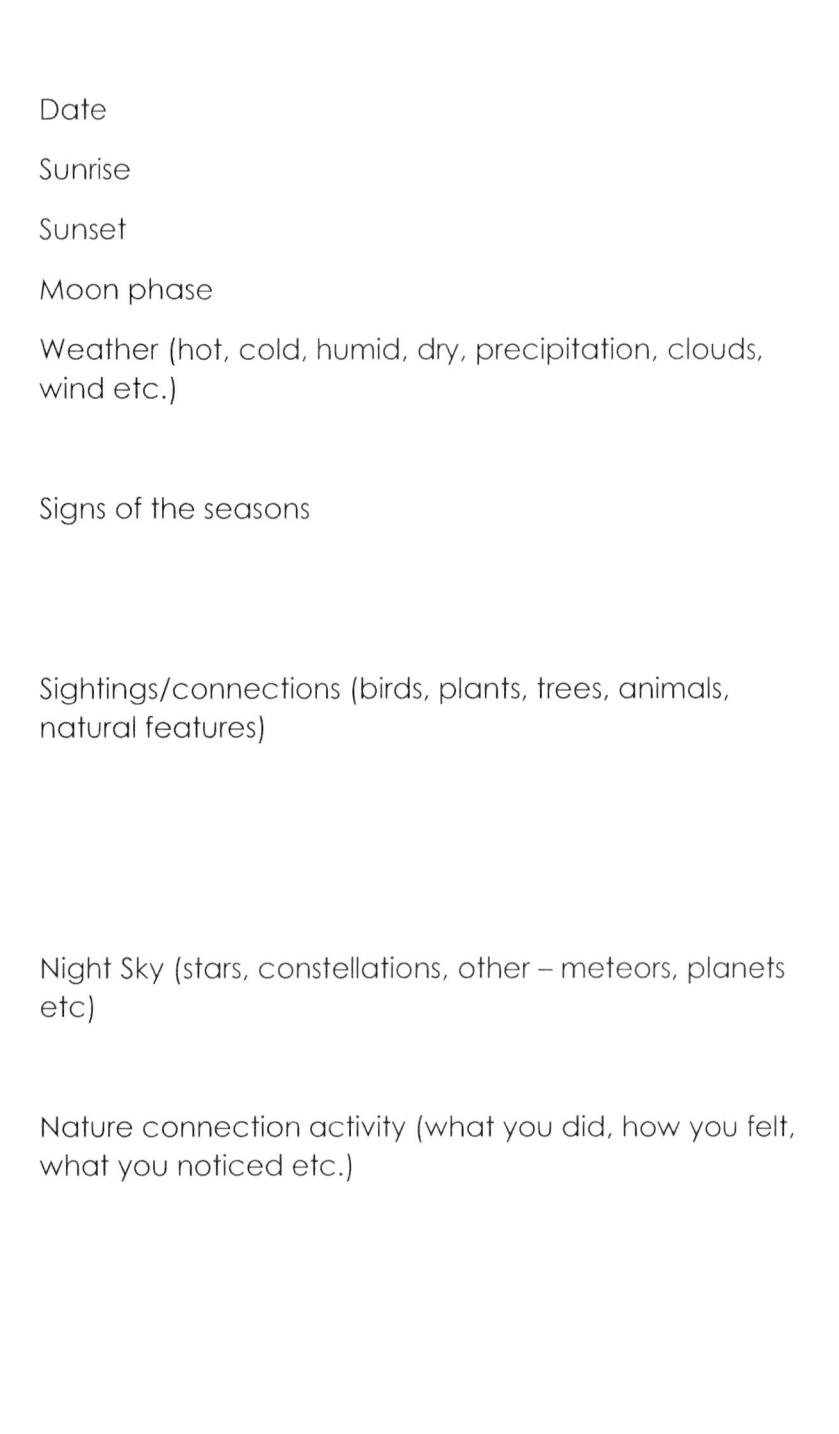

Drawings, pictures, stories, poems, extra notes, gratitudes, ways I gave service to nature

Date

Sunrise

Sunset

Moon phase

Weather (hot, cold, humid, dry, precipitation, clouds, wind etc.)

Signs of the seasons

Sightings/connections (birds, plants, trees, animals, natural features)

Night Sky (stars, constellations, other – meteors, planets etc)

Nature connection activity (what you did, how you felt, what you noticed etc.)

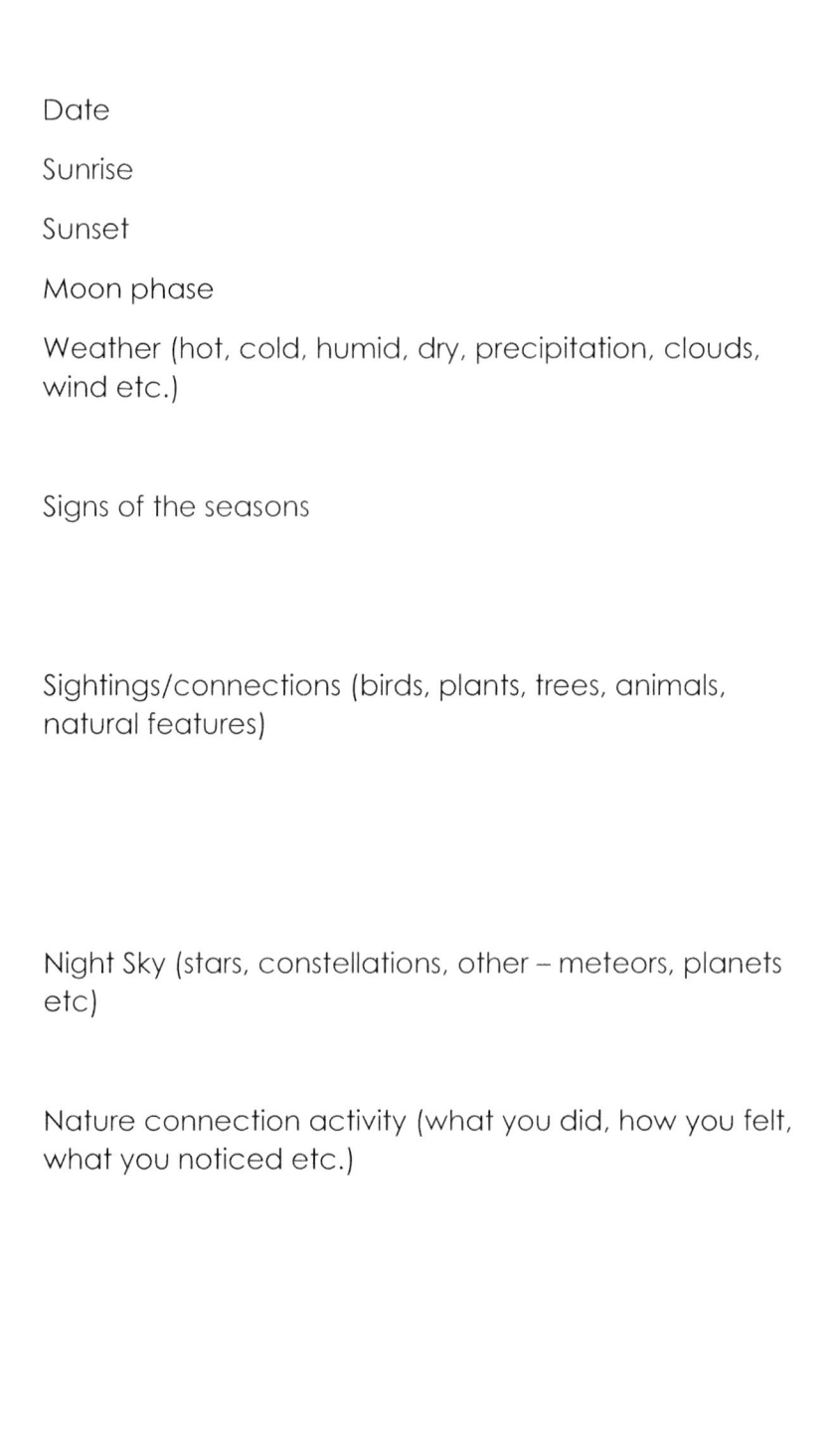

Drawings, pictures, stories, poems, extra notes, gratitudes, ways I gave service to nature

Date

Sunrise

Sunset

Moon phase

Weather (hot, cold, humid, dry, precipitation, clouds, wind etc.)

Signs of the seasons

Sightings/connections (birds, plants, trees, animals, natural features)

Night Sky (stars, constellations, other – meteors, planets etc)

Nature connection activity (what you did, how you felt, what you noticed etc.)

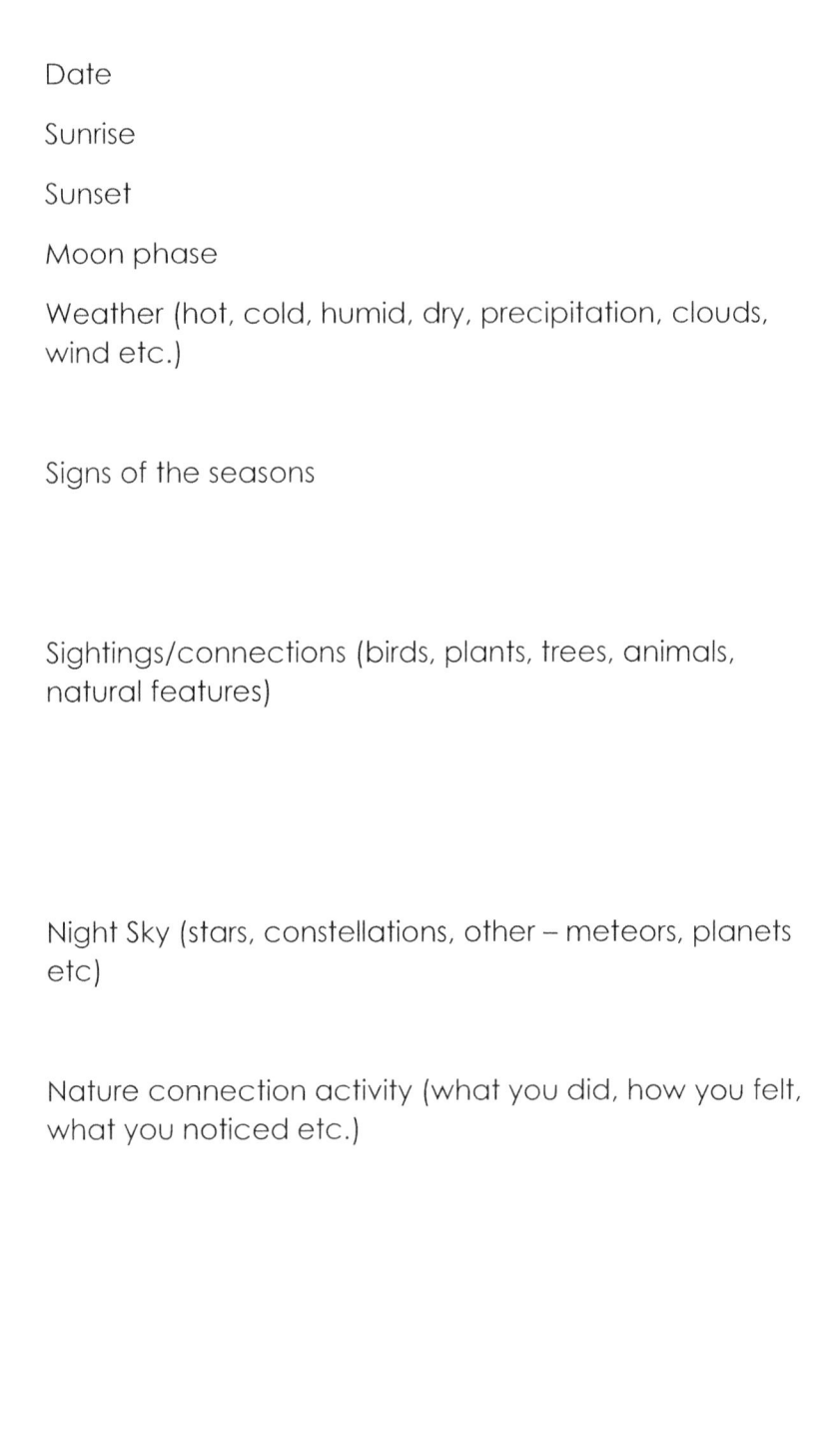

Drawings, pictures, stories, poems, extra notes, gratitudes, ways I gave service to nature

Date

Sunrise

Sunset

Moon phase

Weather (hot, cold, humid, dry, precipitation, clouds, wind etc.)

Signs of the seasons

Sightings/connections (birds, plants, trees, animals, natural features)

Night Sky (stars, constellations, other – meteors, planets etc)

Nature connection activity (what you did, how you felt, what you noticed etc.)

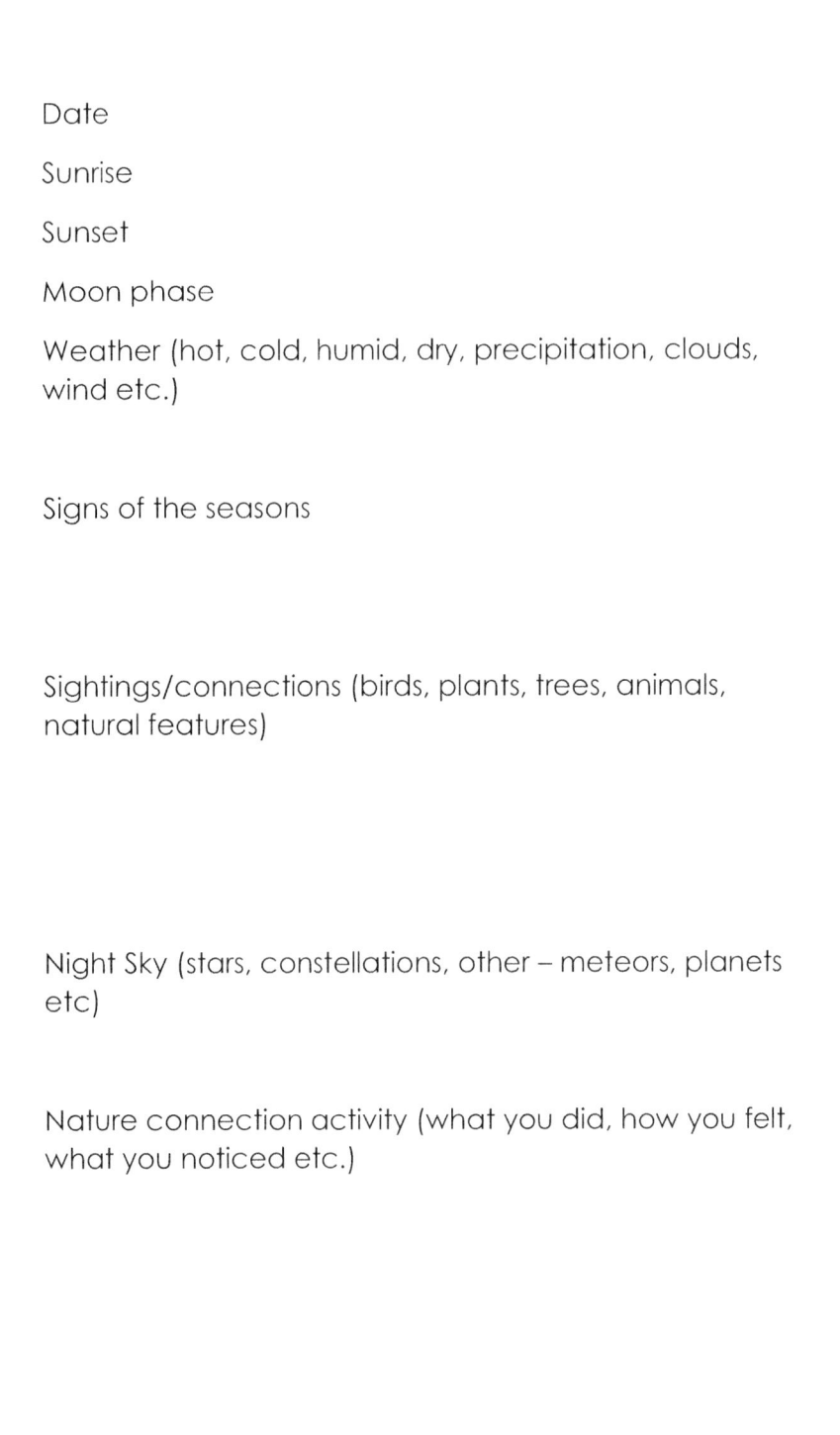

Drawings, pictures, stories, poems, extra notes, gratitudes, ways I gave service to nature

Date

Sunrise

Sunset

Moon phase

Weather (hot, cold, humid, dry, precipitation, clouds, wind etc.)

Signs of the seasons

Sightings/connections (birds, plants, trees, animals, natural features)

Night Sky (stars, constellations, other – meteors, planets etc)

Nature connection activity (what you did, how you felt, what you noticed etc.)

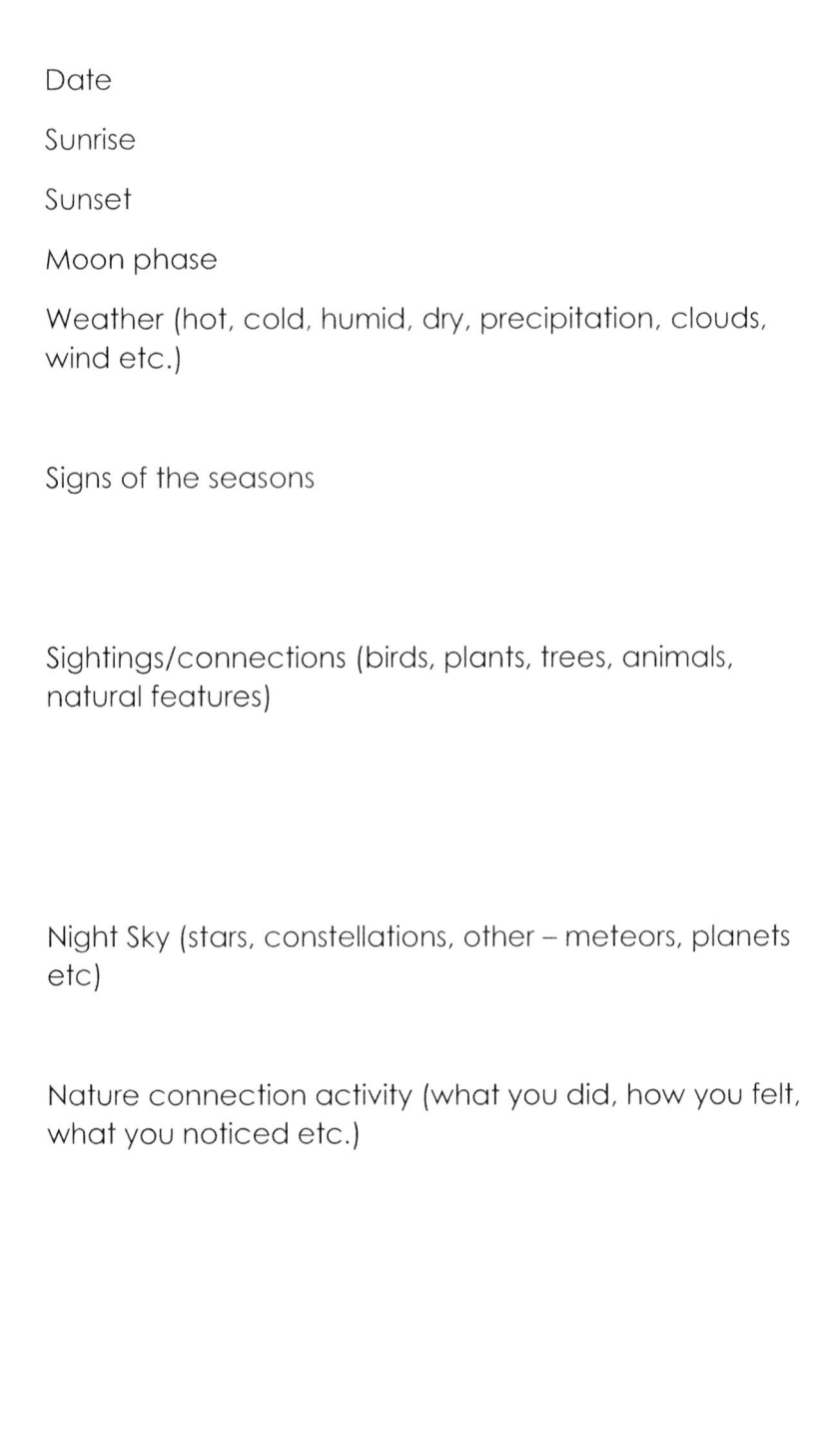

Drawings, pictures, stories, poems, extra notes, gratitudes, ways I gave service to nature

Date

Sunrise

Sunset

Moon phase

Weather (hot, cold, humid, dry, precipitation, clouds, wind etc.)

Signs of the seasons

Sightings/connections (birds, plants, trees, animals, natural features)

Night Sky (stars, constellations, other – meteors, planets etc)

Nature connection activity (what you did, how you felt, what you noticed etc.)

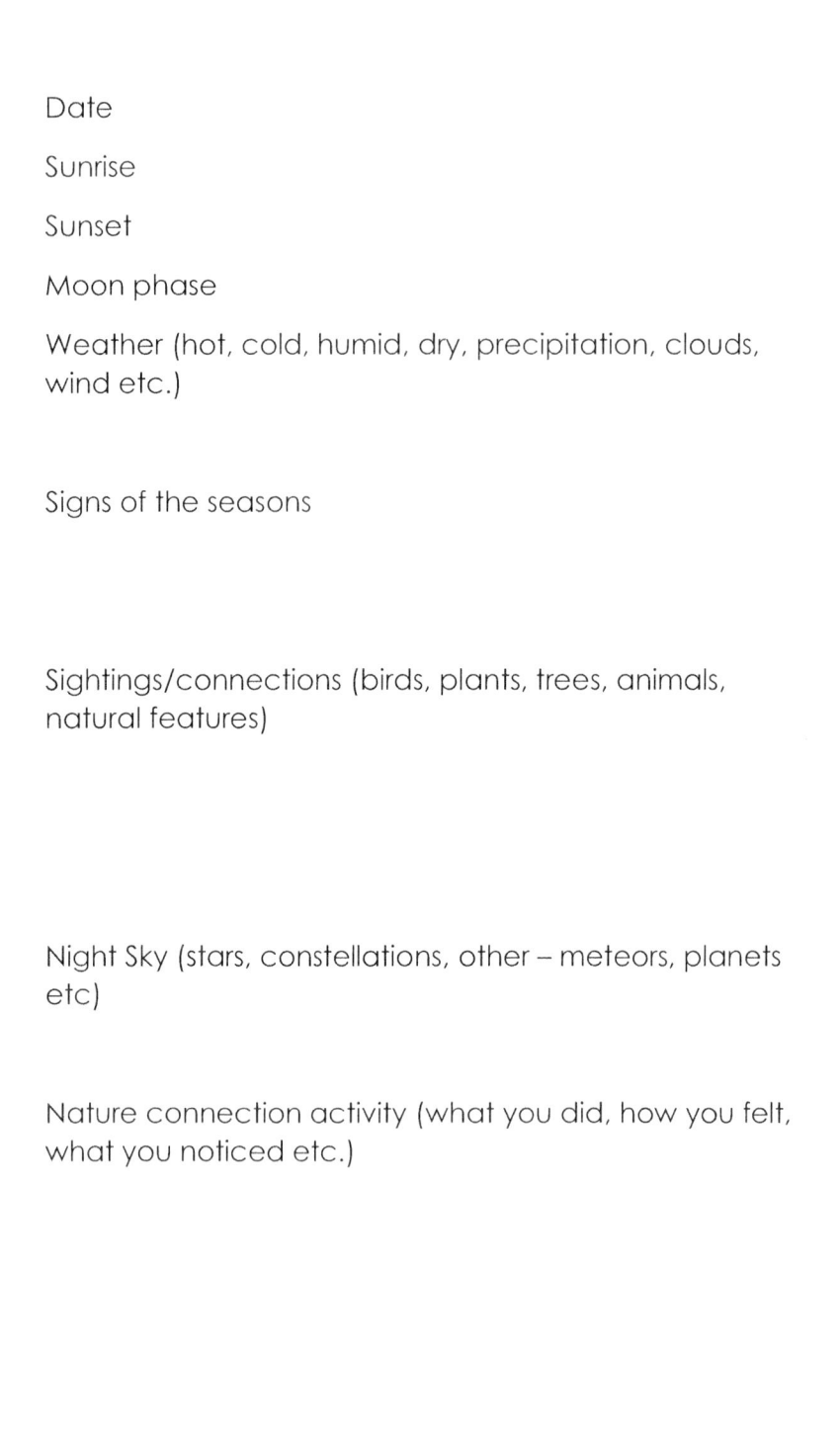

Drawings, pictures, stories, poems, extra notes, gratitudes, ways I gave service to nature

Date

Sunrise

Sunset

Moon phase

Weather (hot, cold, humid, dry, precipitation, clouds, wind etc.)

Signs of the seasons

Sightings/connections (birds, plants, trees, animals, natural features)

Night Sky (stars, constellations, other – meteors, planets etc)

Nature connection activity (what you did, how you felt, what you noticed etc.)

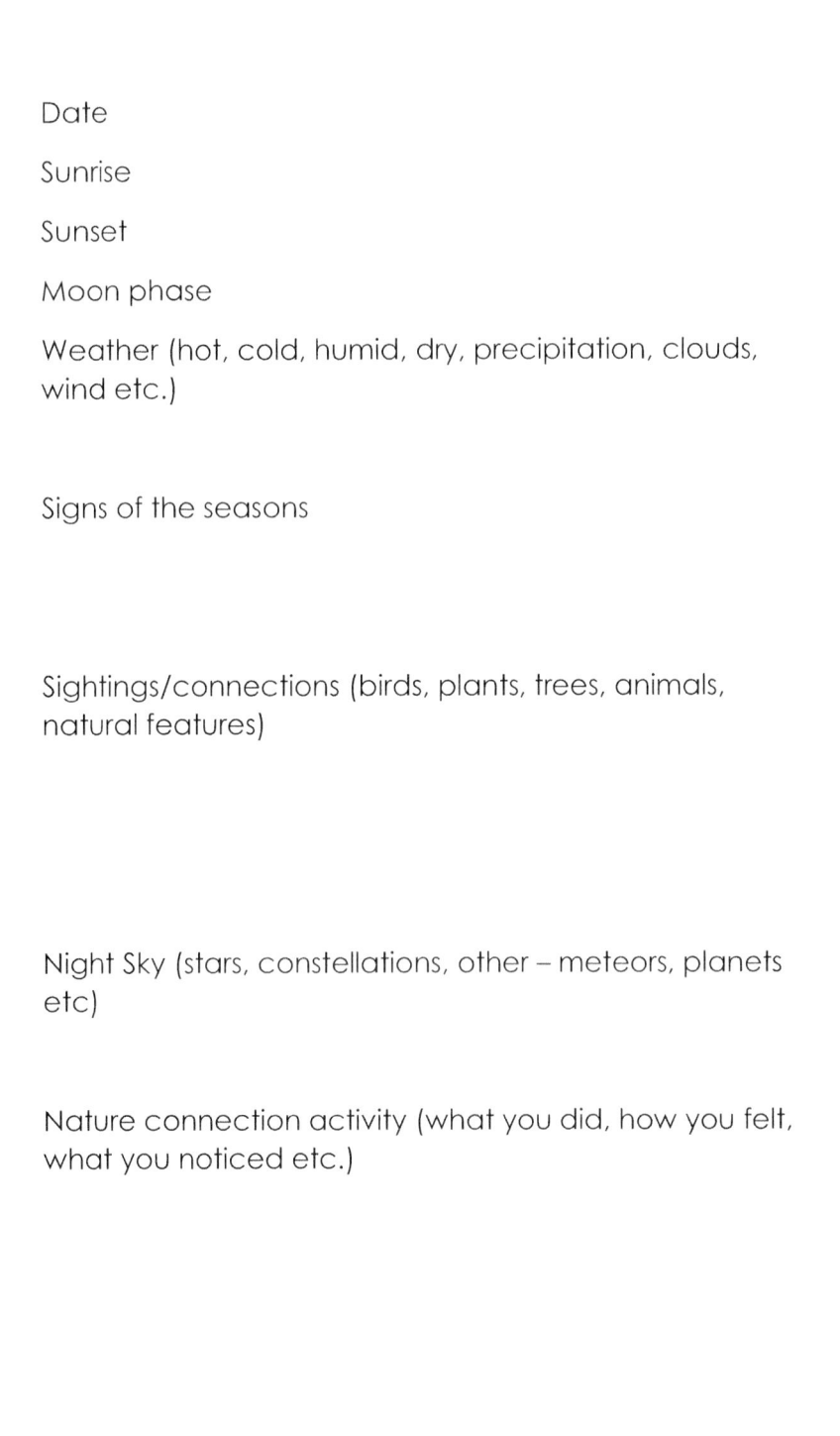

Drawings, pictures, stories, poems, extra notes, gratitudes, ways I gave service to nature

Date

Sunrise

Sunset

Moon phase

Weather (hot, cold, humid, dry, precipitation, clouds, wind etc.)

Signs of the seasons

Sightings/connections (birds, plants, trees, animals, natural features)

Night Sky (stars, constellations, other – meteors, planets etc)

Nature connection activity (what you did, how you felt, what you noticed etc.)

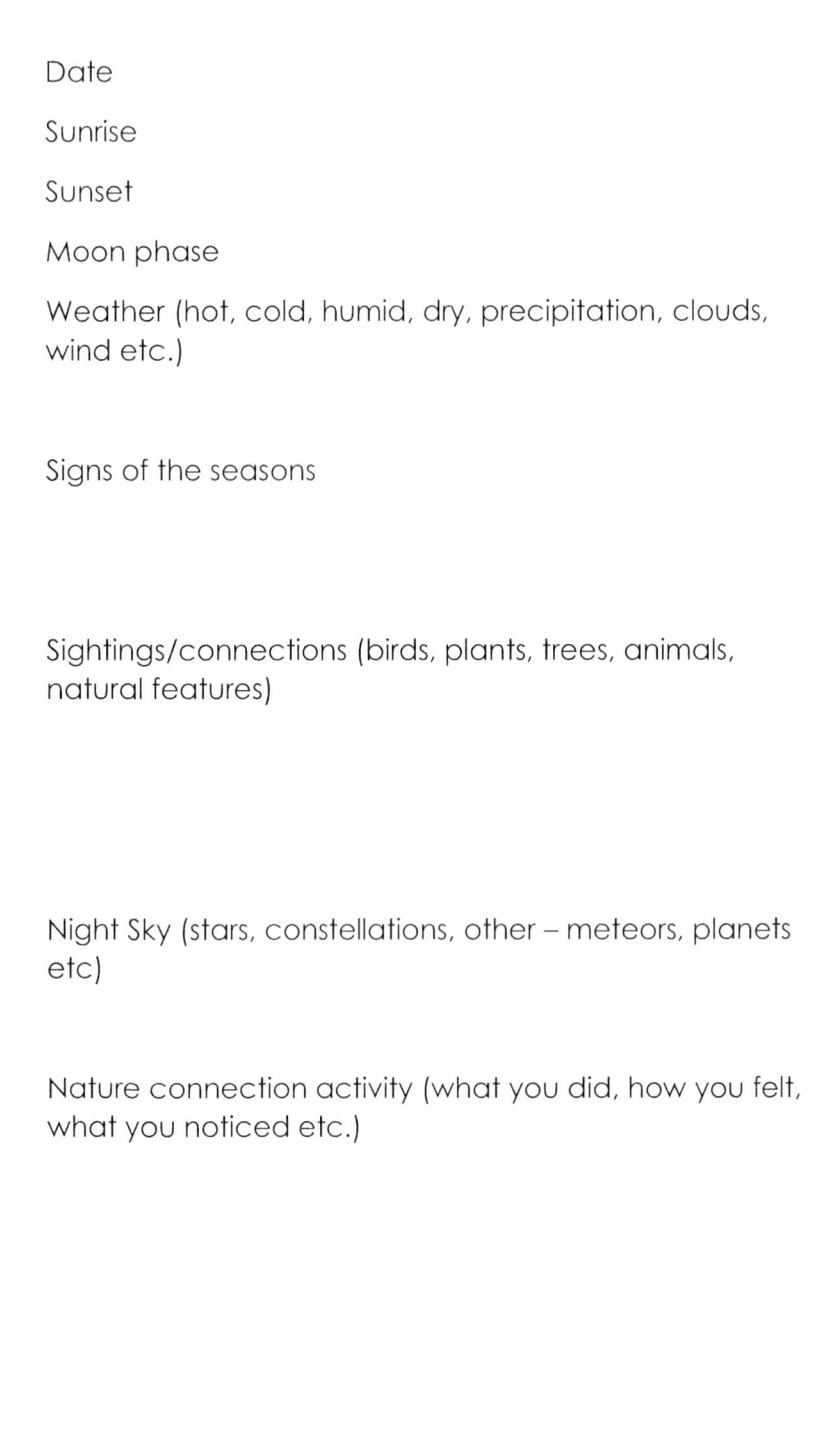

Drawings, pictures, stories, poems, extra notes, gratitudes, ways I gave service to nature

Date

Sunrise

Sunset

Moon phase

Weather (hot, cold, humid, dry, precipitation, clouds, wind etc.)

Signs of the seasons

Sightings/connections (birds, plants, trees, animals, natural features)

Night Sky (stars, constellations, other – meteors, planets etc)

Nature connection activity (what you did, how you felt, what you noticed etc.)

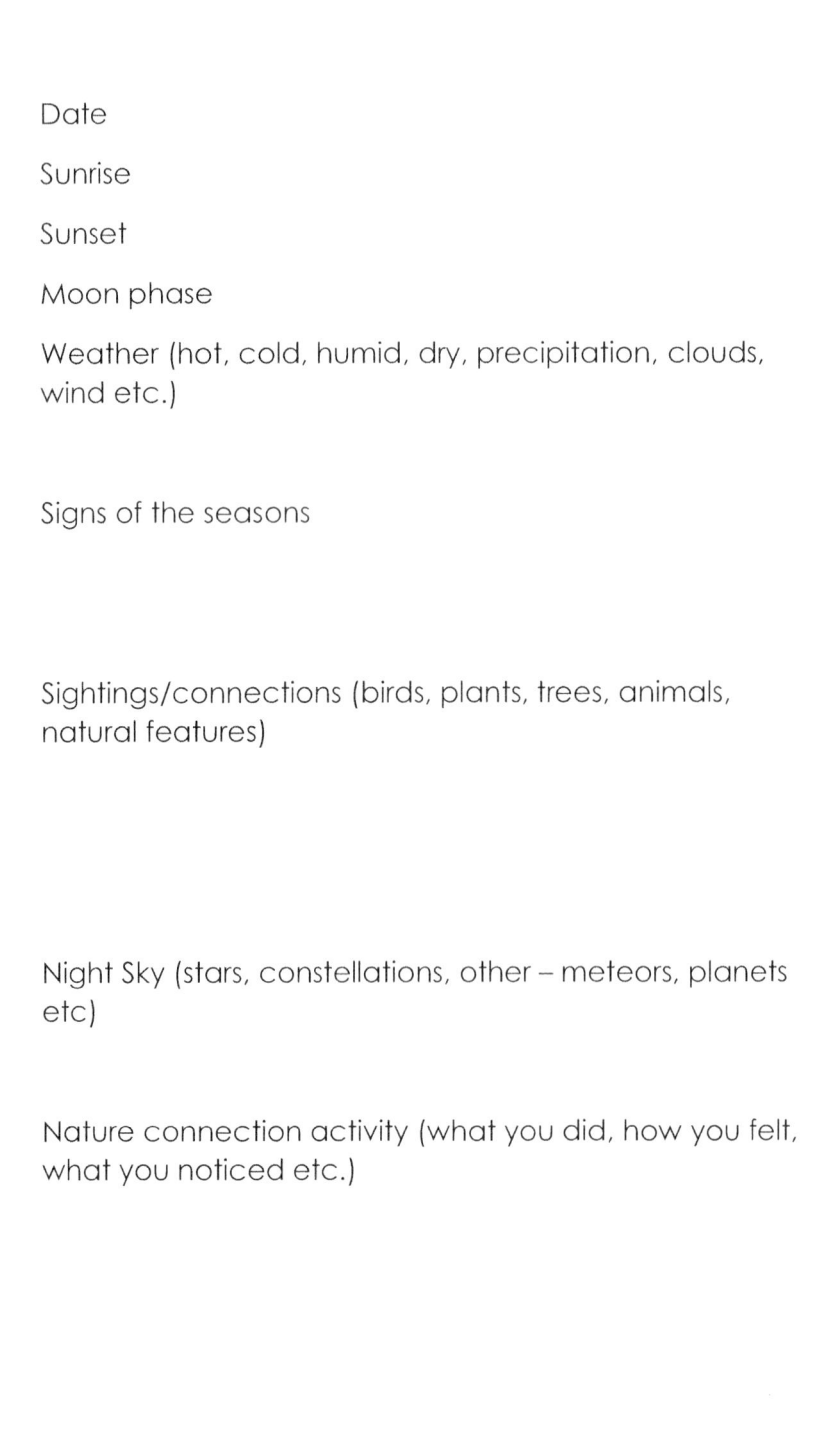

Drawings, pictures, stories, poems, extra notes, gratitudes, ways I gave service to nature

Date

Sunrise

Sunset

Moon phase

Weather (hot, cold, humid, dry, precipitation, clouds, wind etc.)

Signs of the seasons

Sightings/connections (birds, plants, trees, animals, natural features)

Night Sky (stars, constellations, other – meteors, planets etc)

Nature connection activity (what you did, how you felt, what you noticed etc.)

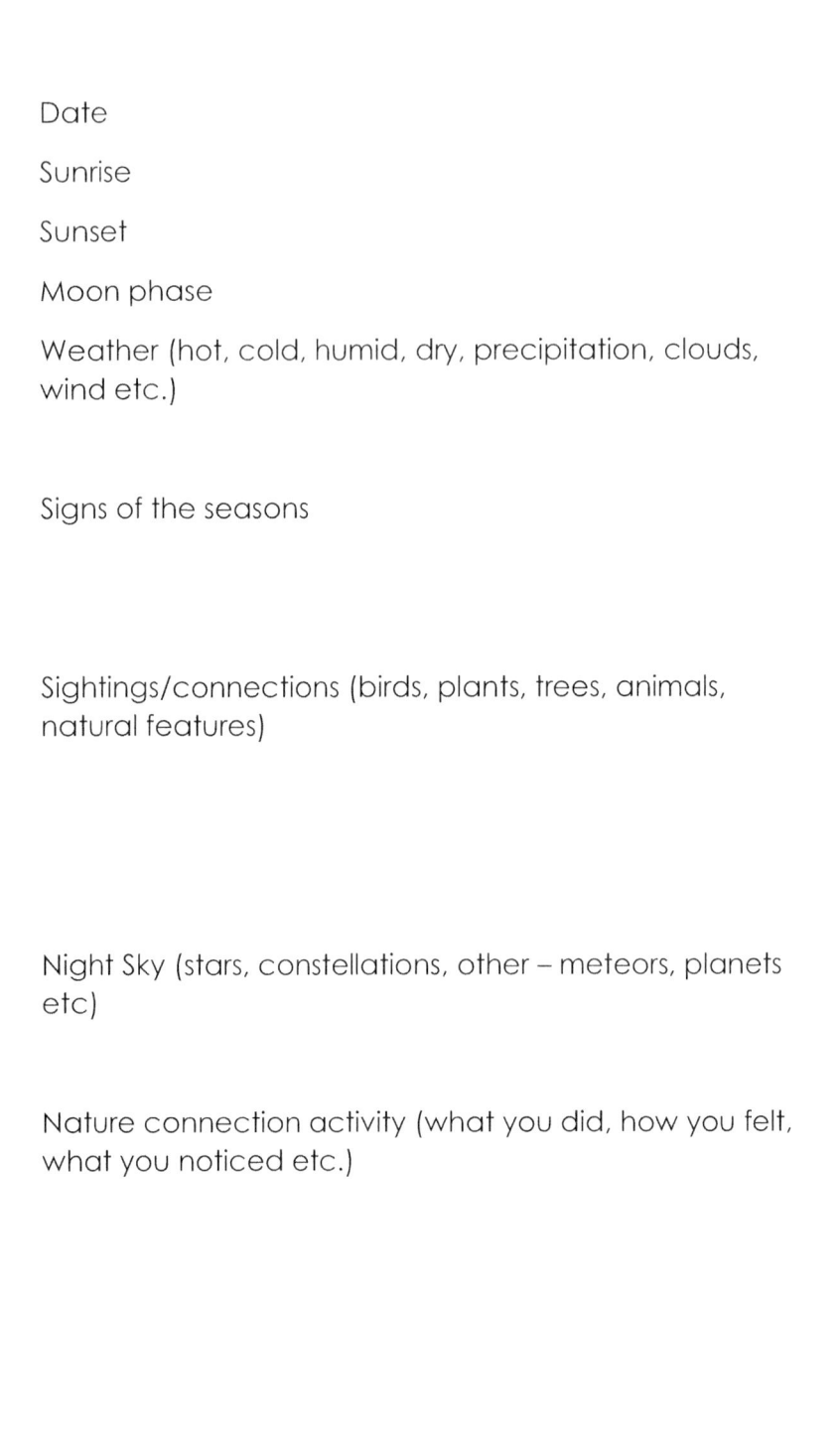

Drawings, pictures, stories, poems, extra notes, gratitudes, ways I gave service to nature

Date

Sunrise

Sunset

Moon phase

Weather (hot, cold, humid, dry, precipitation, clouds, wind etc.)

Signs of the seasons

Sightings/connections (birds, plants, trees, animals, natural features)

Night Sky (stars, constellations, other – meteors, planets etc)

Nature connection activity (what you did, how you felt, what you noticed etc.)

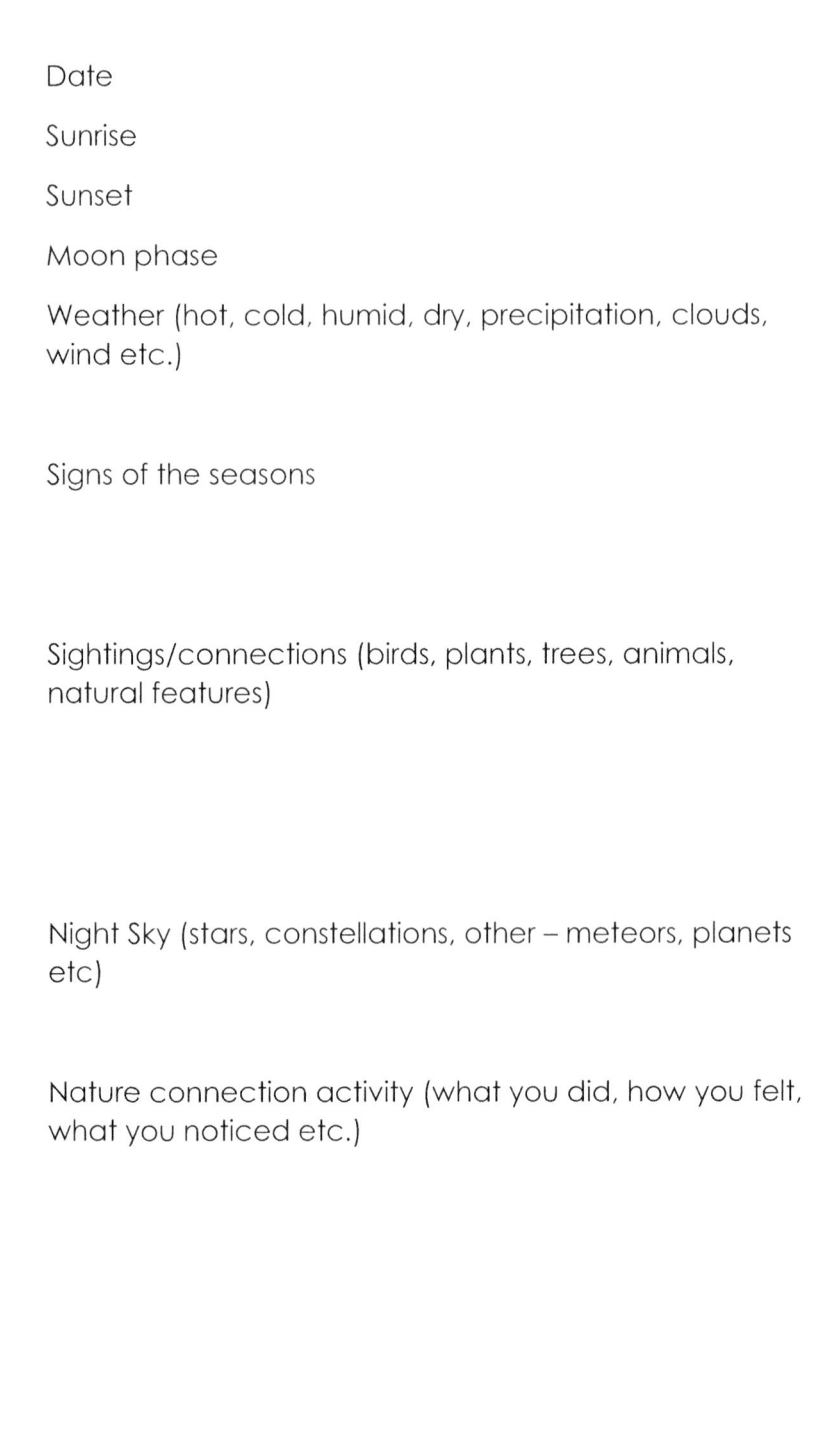

Drawings, pictures, stories, poems, extra notes, gratitudes, ways I gave service to nature

Date

Sunrise

Sunset

Moon phase

Weather (hot, cold, humid, dry, precipitation, clouds, wind etc.)

Signs of the seasons

Sightings/connections (birds, plants, trees, animals, natural features)

Night Sky (stars, constellations, other – meteors, planets etc)

Nature connection activity (what you did, how you felt, what you noticed etc.)

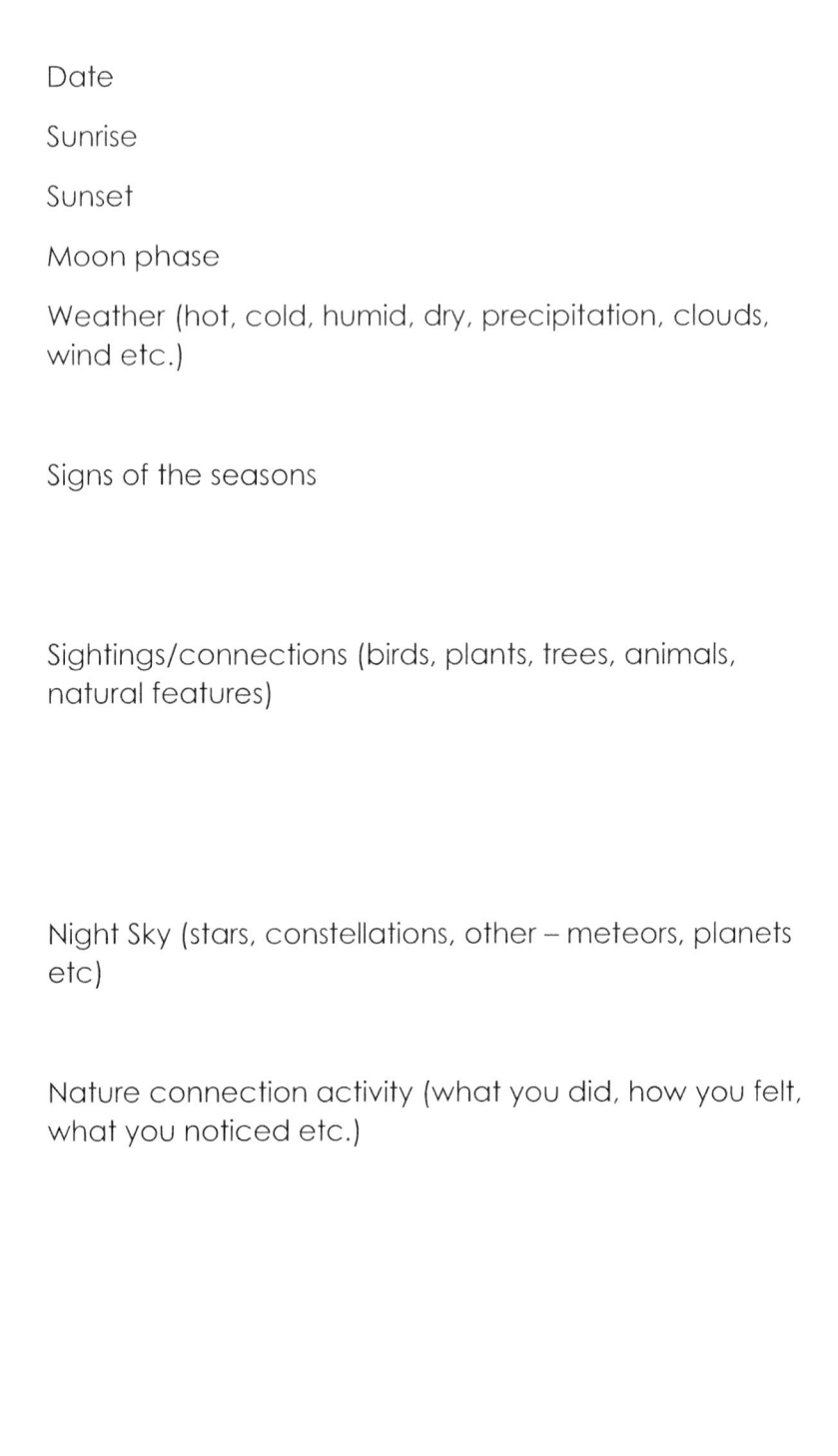

Drawings, pictures, stories, poems, extra notes, gratitudes, ways I gave service to nature

Date

Sunrise

Sunset

Moon phase

Weather (hot, cold, humid, dry, precipitation, clouds, wind etc.)

Signs of the seasons

Sightings/connections (birds, plants, trees, animals, natural features)

Night Sky (stars, constellations, other – meteors, planets etc)

Nature connection activity (what you did, how you felt, what you noticed etc.)

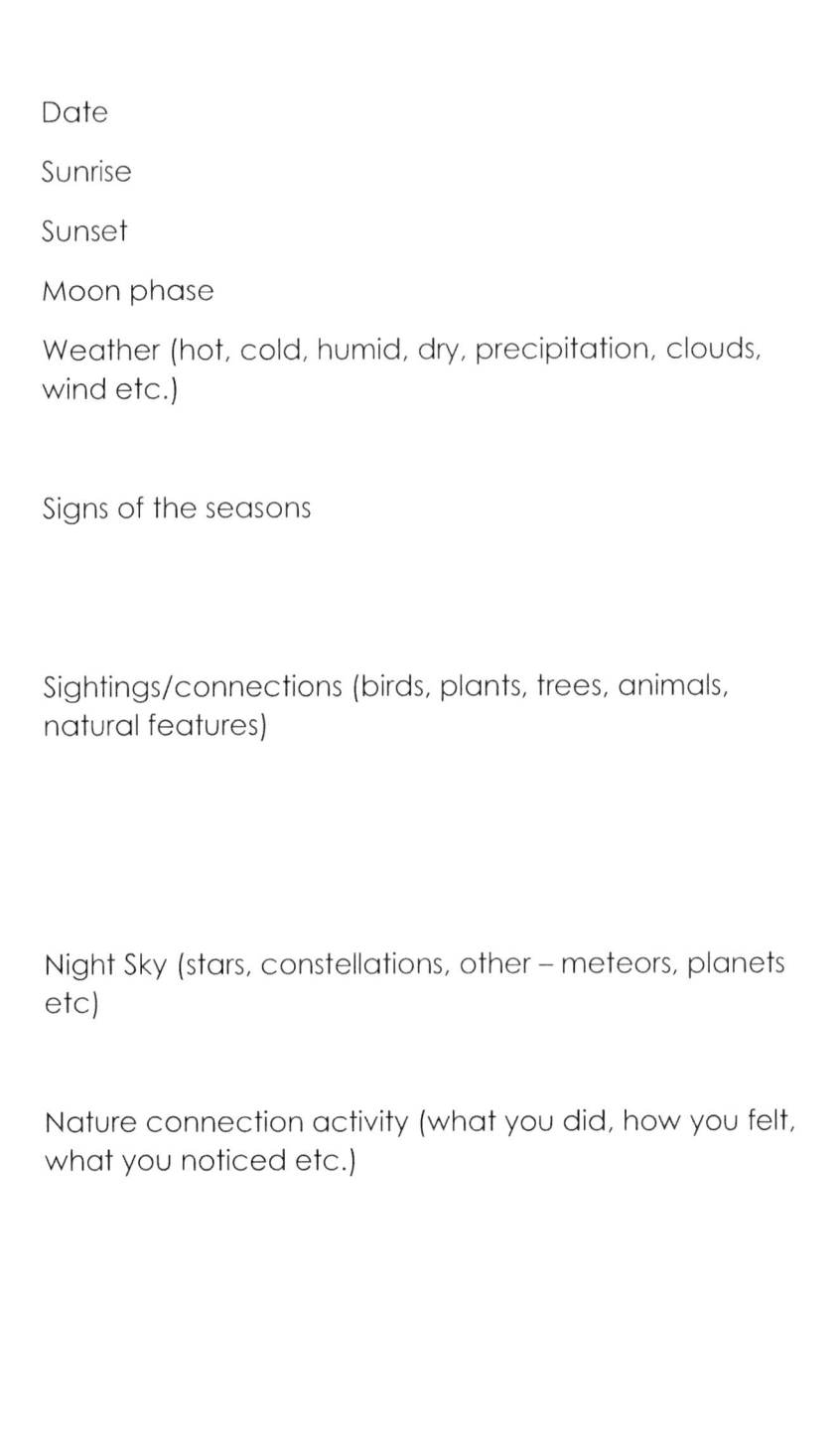

Drawings, pictures, stories, poems, extra notes, gratitudes, ways I gave service to nature

Date

Sunrise

Sunset

Moon phase

Weather (hot, cold, humid, dry, precipitation, clouds, wind etc.)

Signs of the seasons

Sightings/connections (birds, plants, trees, animals, natural features)

Night Sky (stars, constellations, other – meteors, planets etc)

Nature connection activity (what you did, how you felt, what you noticed etc.)

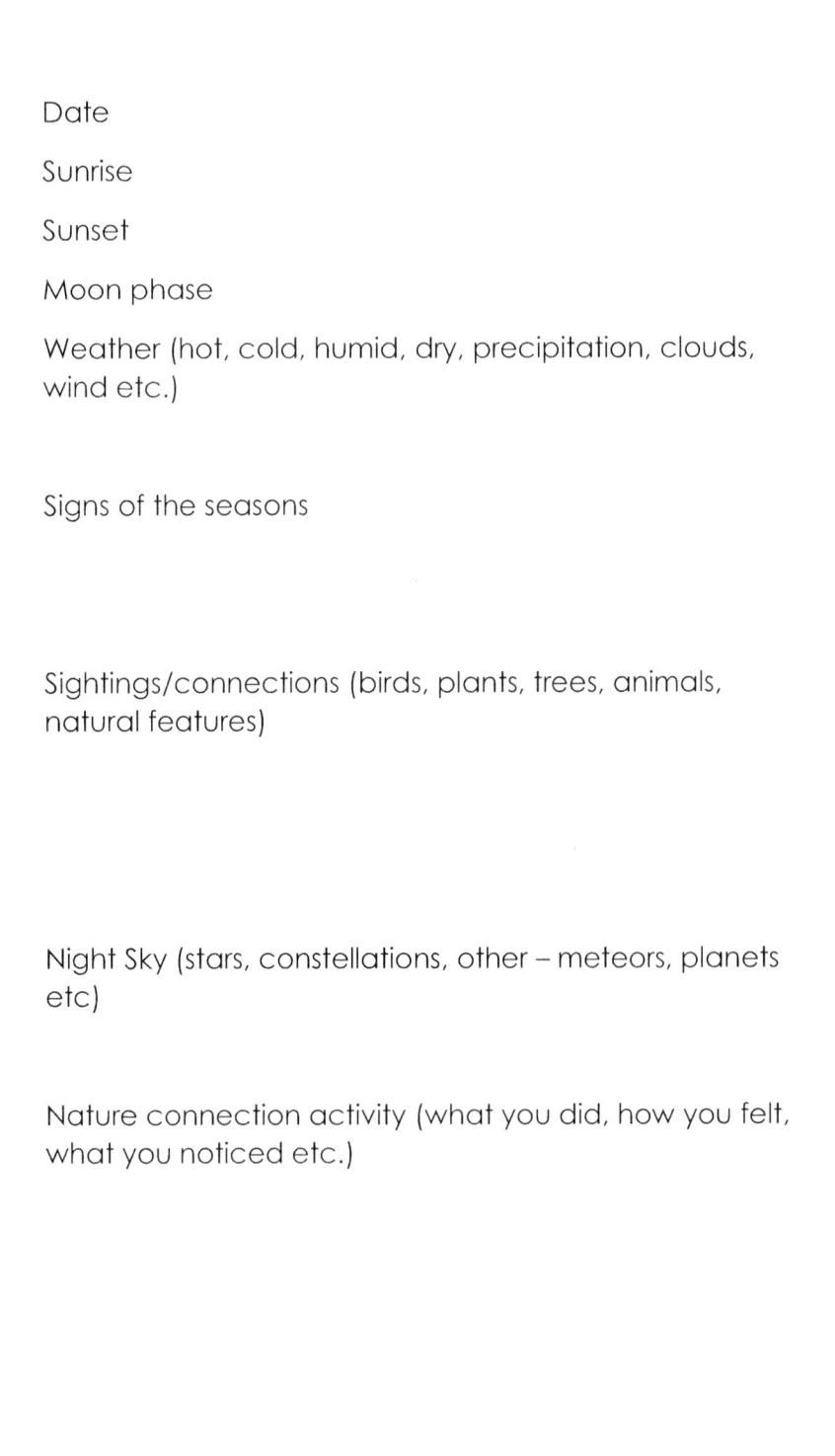

Drawings, pictures, stories, poems, extra notes, gratitudes, ways I gave service to nature

Date

Sunrise

Sunset

Moon phase

Weather (hot, cold, humid, dry, precipitation, clouds, wind etc.)

Signs of the seasons

Sightings/connections (birds, plants, trees, animals, natural features)

Night Sky (stars, constellations, other – meteors, planets etc)

Nature connection activity (what you did, how you felt, what you noticed etc.)

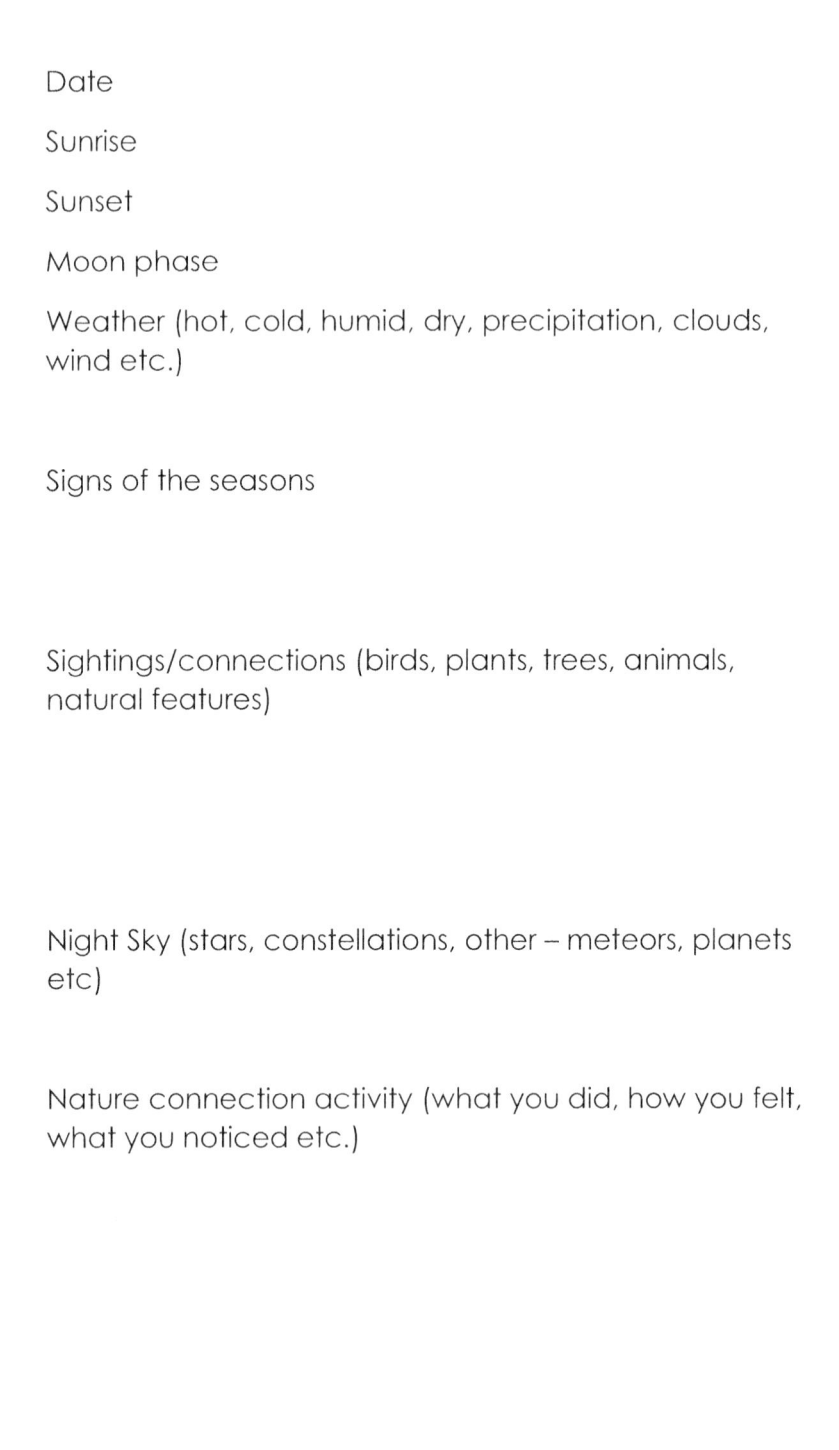

Drawings, pictures, stories, poems, extra notes, gratitudes, ways I gave service to nature

Date

Sunrise

Sunset

Moon phase

Weather (hot, cold, humid, dry, precipitation, clouds, wind etc.)

Signs of the seasons

Sightings/connections (birds, plants, trees, animals, natural features)

Night Sky (stars, constellations, other – meteors, planets etc)

Nature connection activity (what you did, how you felt, what you noticed etc.)

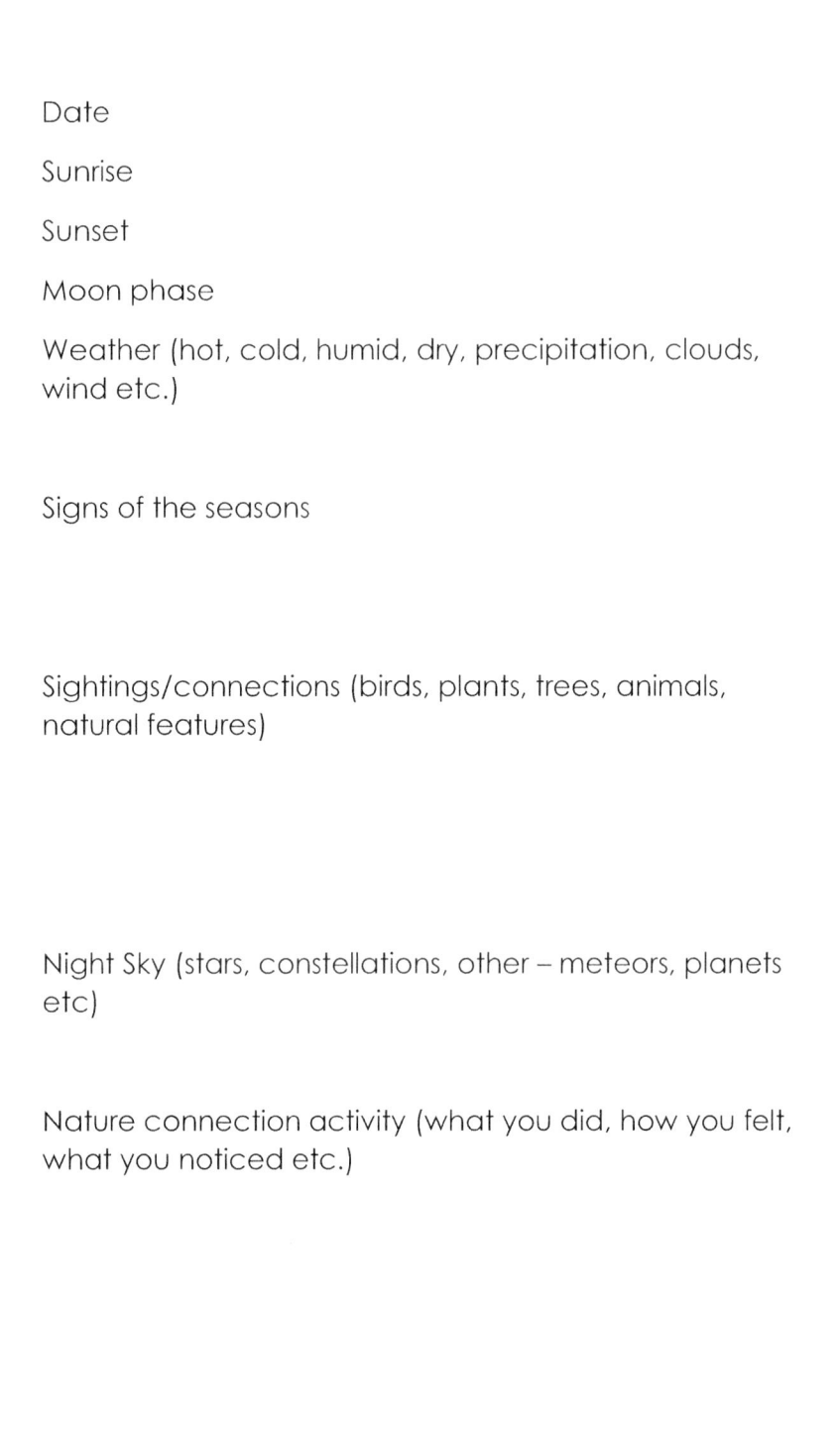

Drawings, pictures, stories, poems, extra notes, gratitudes, ways I gave service to nature

Date

Sunrise

Sunset

Moon phase

Weather (hot, cold, humid, dry, precipitation, clouds, wind etc.)

Signs of the seasons

Sightings/connections (birds, plants, trees, animals, natural features)

Night Sky (stars, constellations, other – meteors, planets etc)

Nature connection activity (what you did, how you felt, what you noticed etc.)

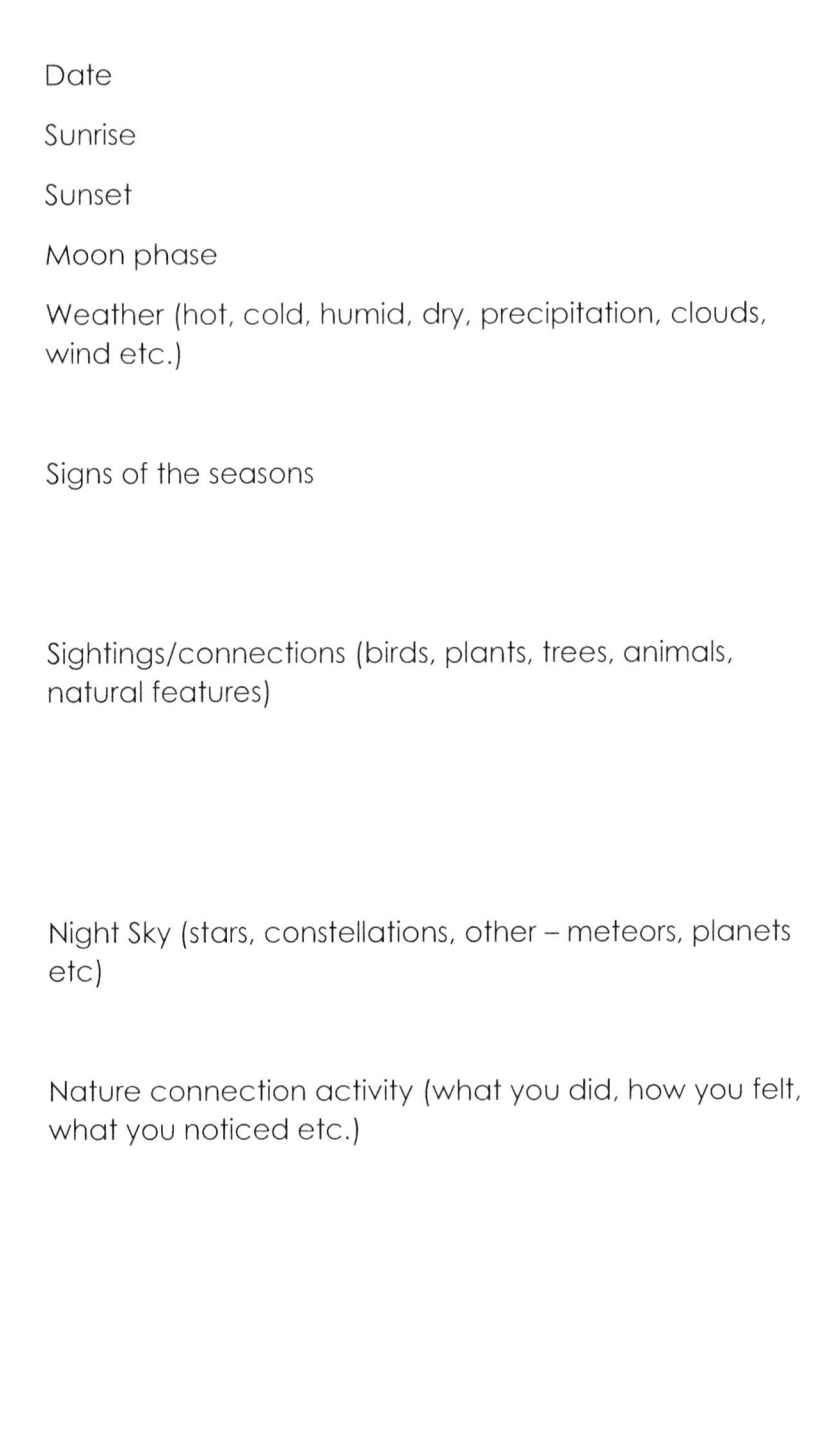

Drawings, pictures, stories, poems, extra notes, gratitudes, ways I gave service to nature

Date

Sunrise

Sunset

Moon phase

Weather (hot, cold, humid, dry, precipitation, clouds, wind etc.)

Signs of the seasons

Sightings/connections (birds, plants, trees, animals, natural features)

Night Sky (stars, constellations, other – meteors, planets etc)

Nature connection activity (what you did, how you felt, what you noticed etc.)

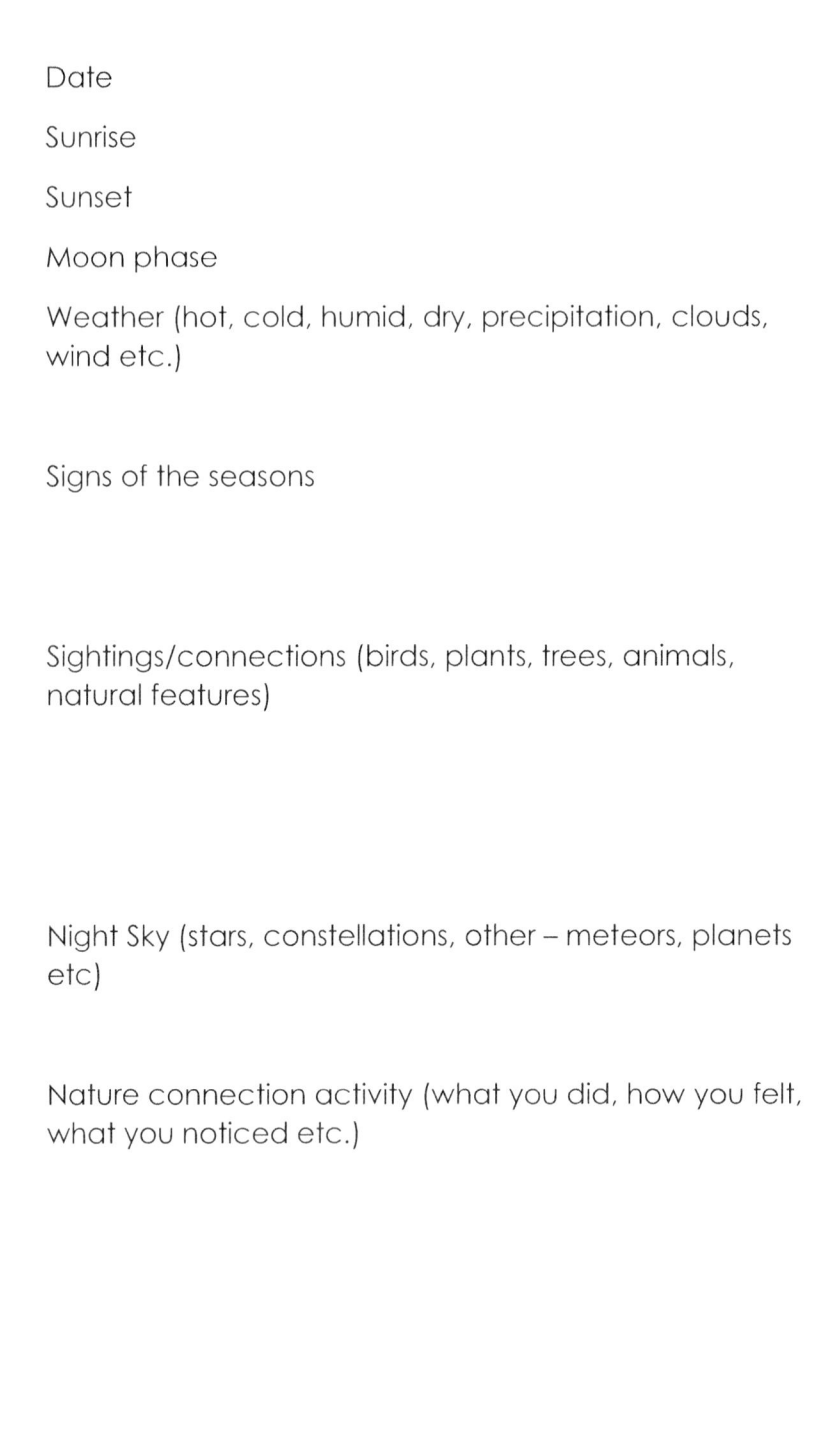

Drawings, pictures, stories, poems, extra notes, gratitudes, ways I gave service to nature

Date

Sunrise

Sunset

Moon phase

Weather (hot, cold, humid, dry, precipitation, clouds, wind etc.)

Signs of the seasons

Sightings/connections (birds, plants, trees, animals, natural features)

Night Sky (stars, constellations, other – meteors, planets etc)

Nature connection activity (what you did, how you felt, what you noticed etc.)

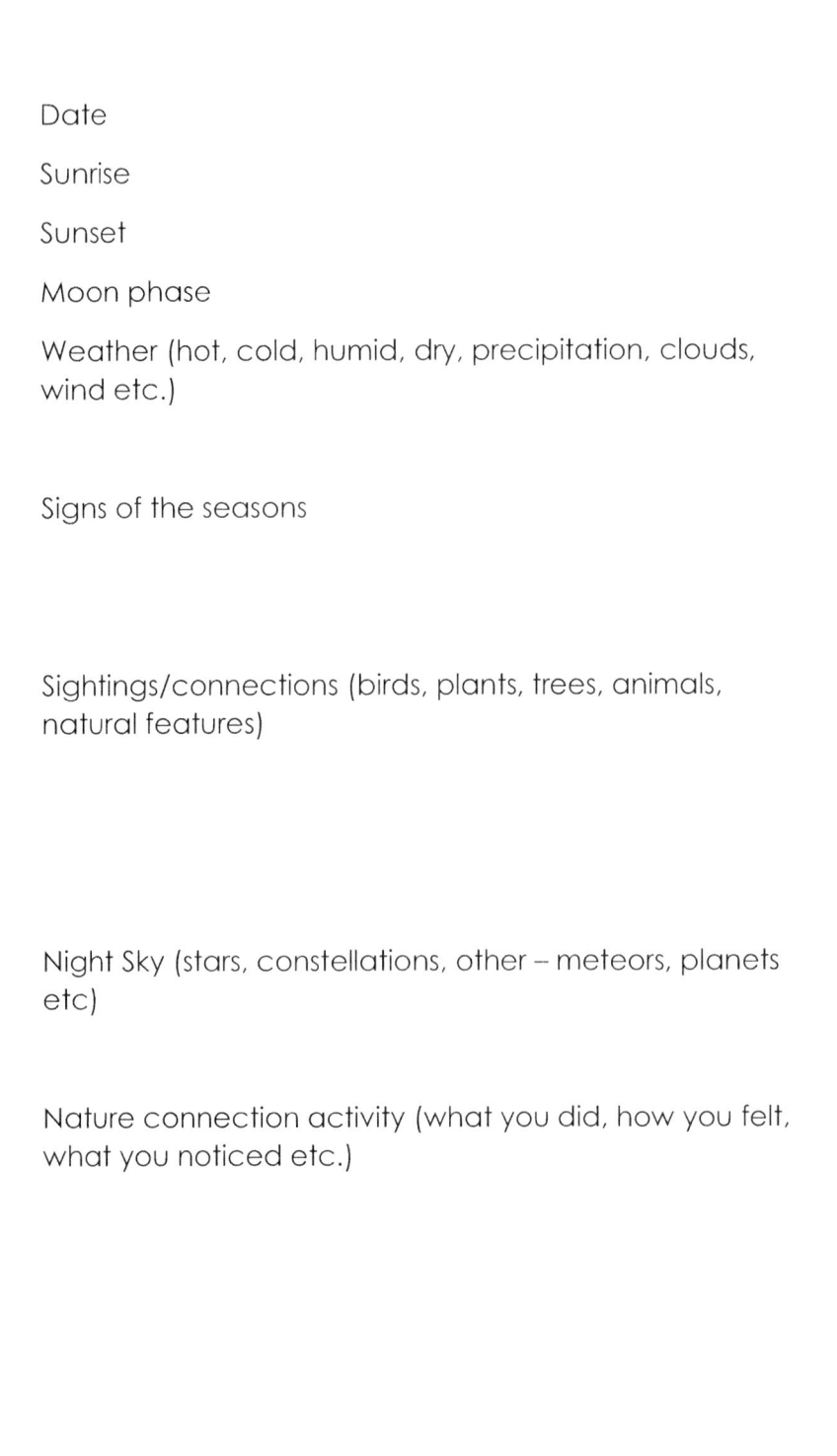

Drawings, pictures, stories, poems, extra notes, gratitudes, ways I gave service to nature

Date

Sunrise

Sunset

Moon phase

Weather (hot, cold, humid, dry, precipitation, clouds, wind etc.)

Signs of the seasons

Sightings/connections (birds, plants, trees, animals, natural features)

Night Sky (stars, constellations, other – meteors, planets etc)

Nature connection activity (what you did, how you felt, what you noticed etc.)

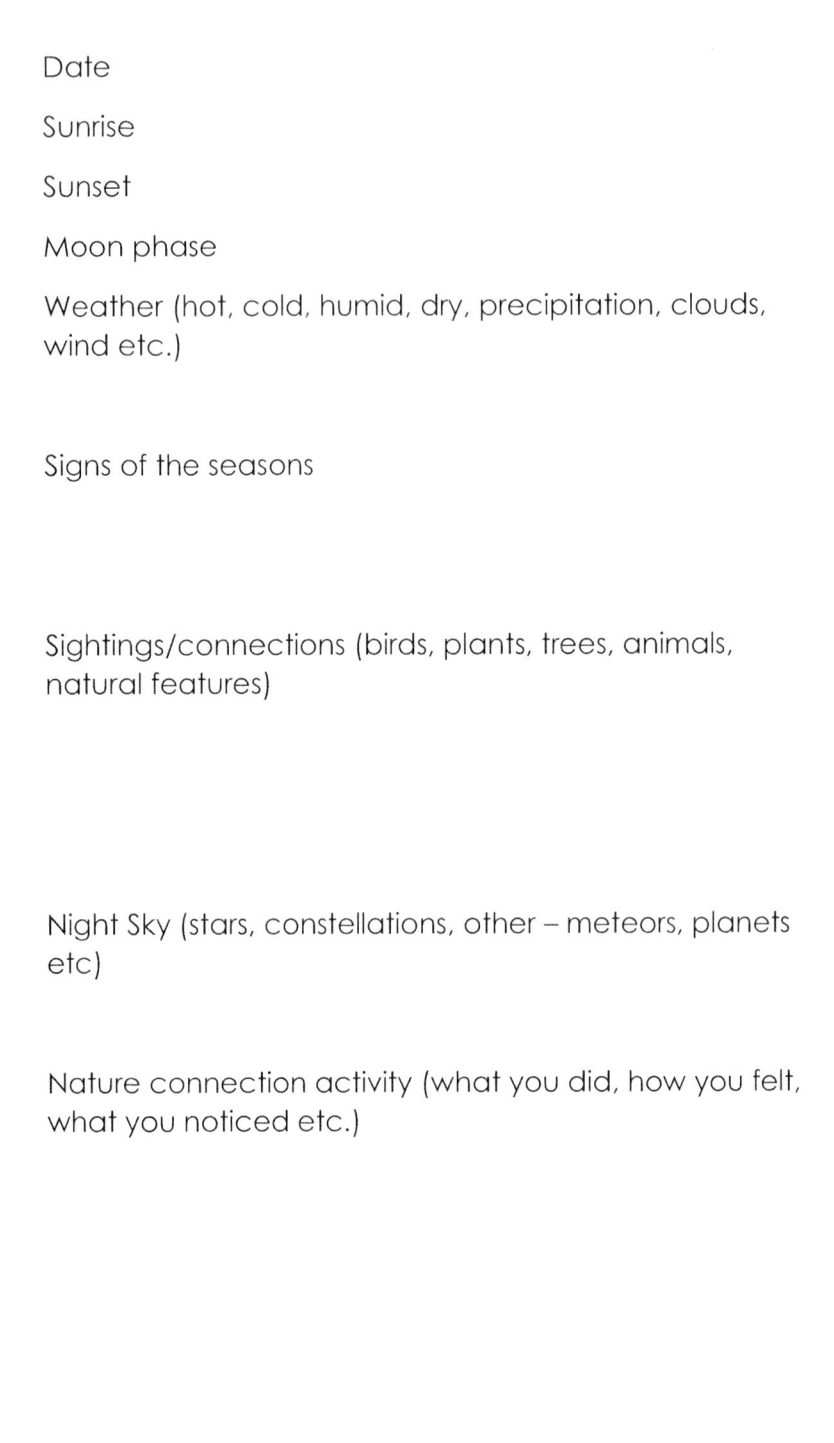

Drawings, pictures, stories, poems, extra notes, gratitudes, ways I gave service to nature

Date

Sunrise

Sunset

Moon phase

Weather (hot, cold, humid, dry, precipitation, clouds, wind etc.)

Signs of the seasons

Sightings/connections (birds, plants, trees, animals, natural features)

Night Sky (stars, constellations, other – meteors, planets etc)

Nature connection activity (what you did, how you felt, what you noticed etc.)

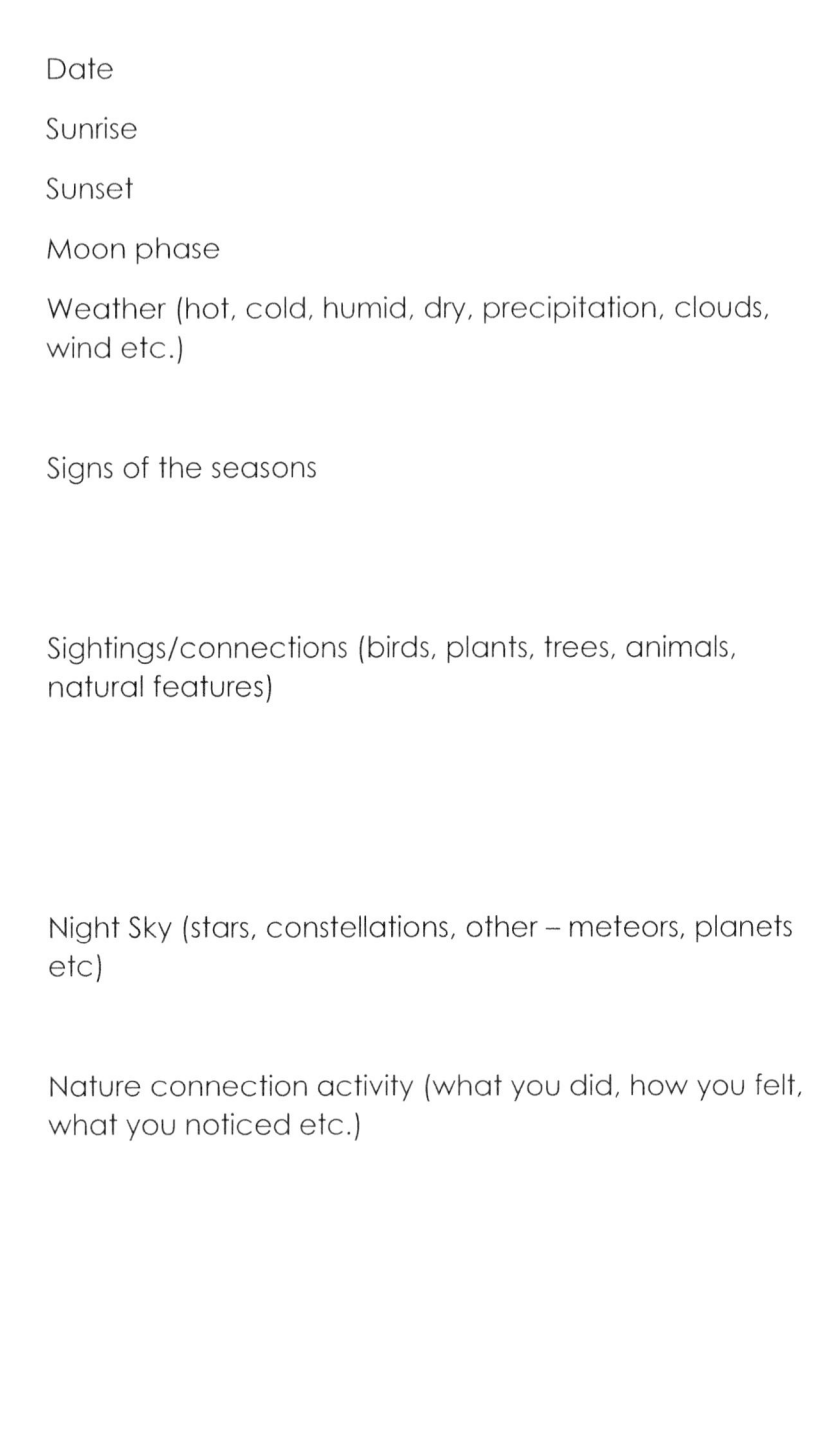

Drawings, pictures, stories, poems, extra notes, gratitudes, ways I gave service to nature

Date

Sunrise

Sunset

Moon phase

Weather (hot, cold, humid, dry, precipitation, clouds, wind etc.)

Signs of the seasons

Sightings/connections (birds, plants, trees, animals, natural features)

Night Sky (stars, constellations, other – meteors, planets etc)

Nature connection activity (what you did, how you felt, what you noticed etc.)

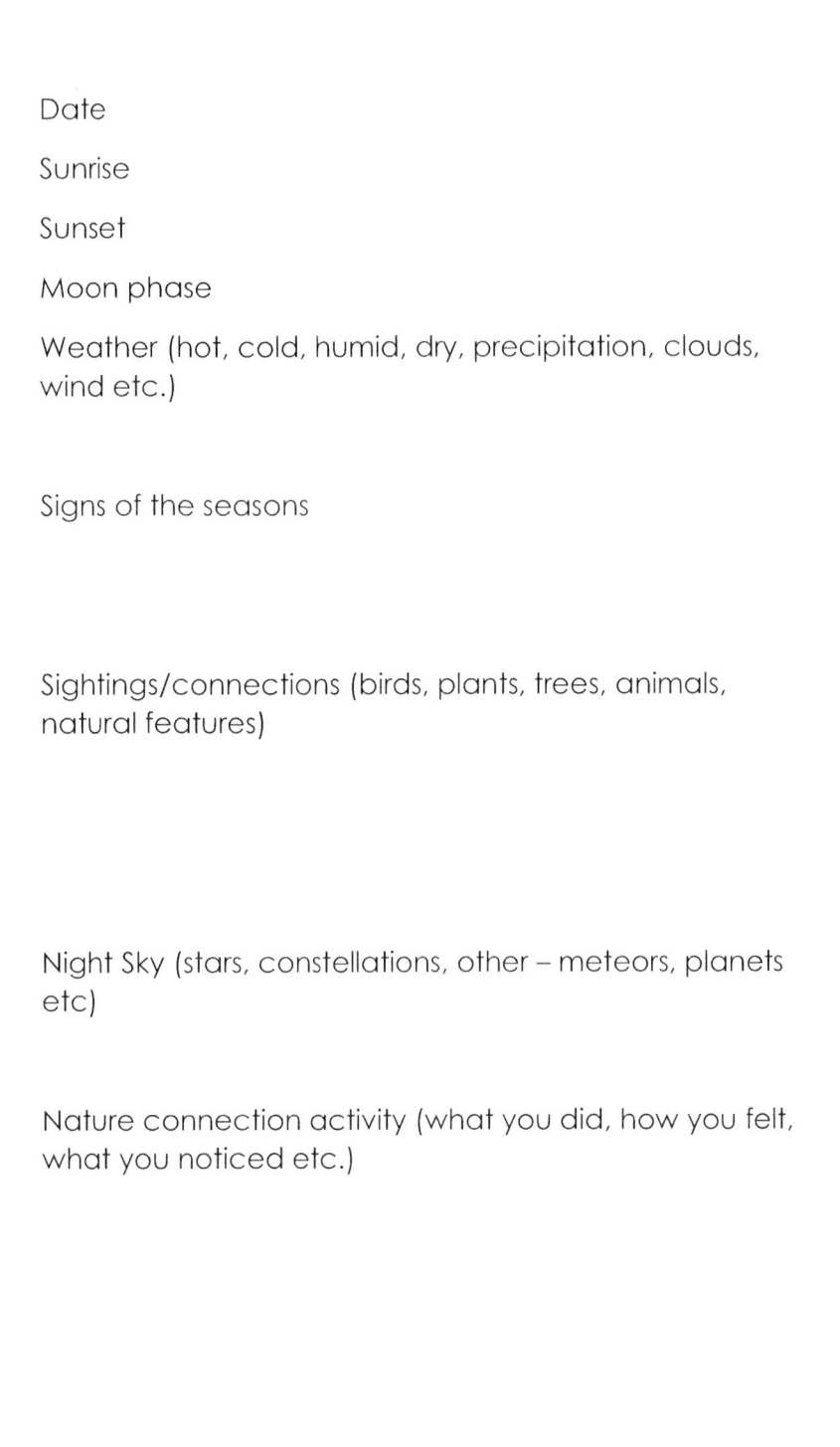

Drawings, pictures, stories, poems, extra notes, gratitudes, ways I gave service to nature

Date

Sunrise

Sunset

Moon phase

Weather (hot, cold, humid, dry, precipitation, clouds, wind etc.)

Signs of the seasons

Sightings/connections (birds, plants, trees, animals, natural features)

Night Sky (stars, constellations, other – meteors, planets etc)

Nature connection activity (what you did, how you felt, what you noticed etc.)

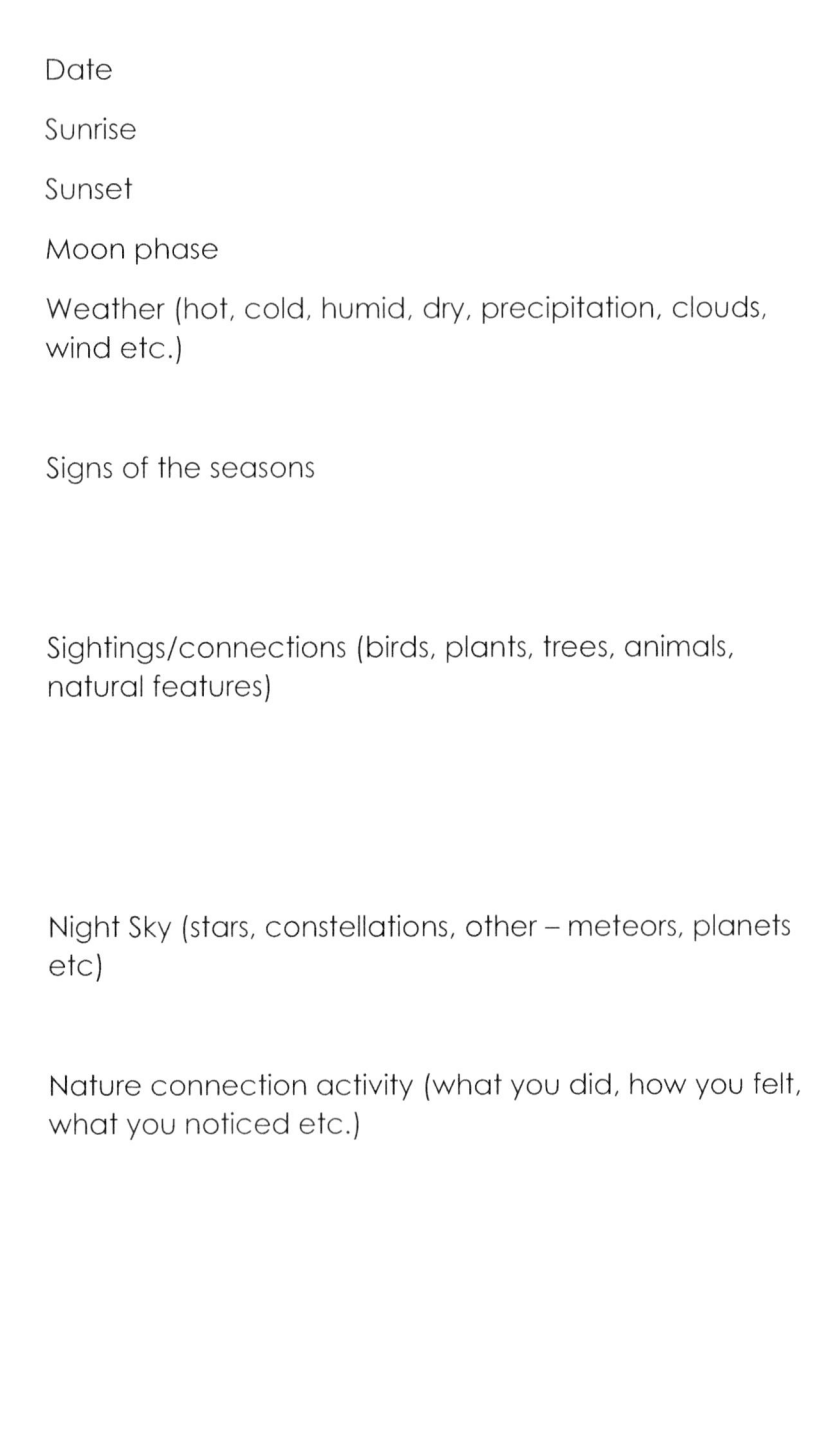

Drawings, pictures, stories, poems, extra notes, gratitudes, ways I gave service to nature

Date

Sunrise

Sunset

Moon phase

Weather (hot, cold, humid, dry, precipitation, clouds, wind etc.)

Signs of the seasons

Sightings/connections (birds, plants, trees, animals, natural features)

Night Sky (stars, constellations, other – meteors, planets etc)

Nature connection activity (what you did, how you felt, what you noticed etc.)

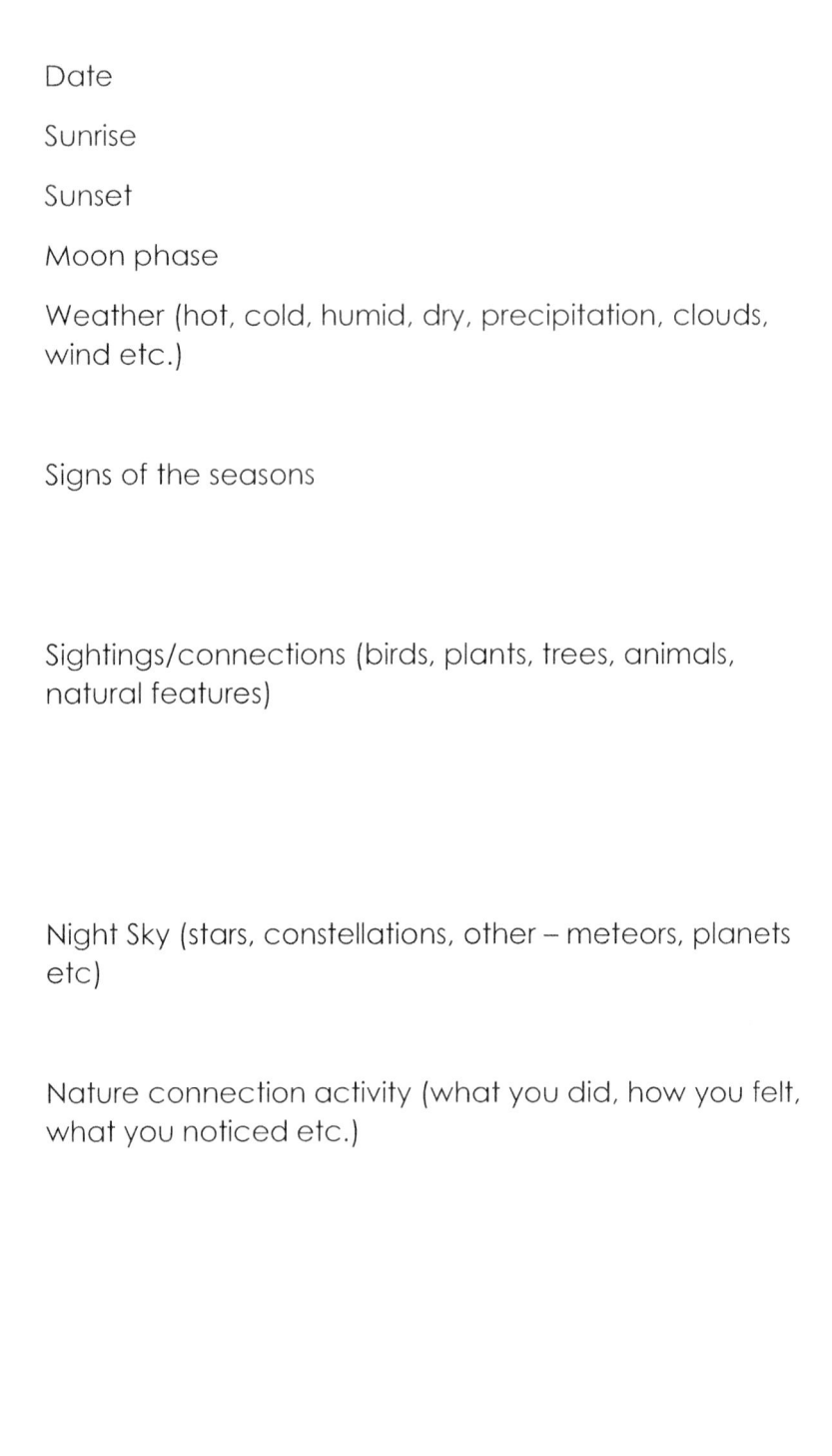

Drawings, pictures, stories, poems, extra notes, gratitudes, ways I gave service to nature

Date

Sunrise

Sunset

Moon phase

Weather (hot, cold, humid, dry, precipitation, clouds, wind etc.)

Signs of the seasons

Sightings/connections (birds, plants, trees, animals, natural features)

Night Sky (stars, constellations, other – meteors, planets etc)

Nature connection activity (what you did, how you felt, what you noticed etc.)

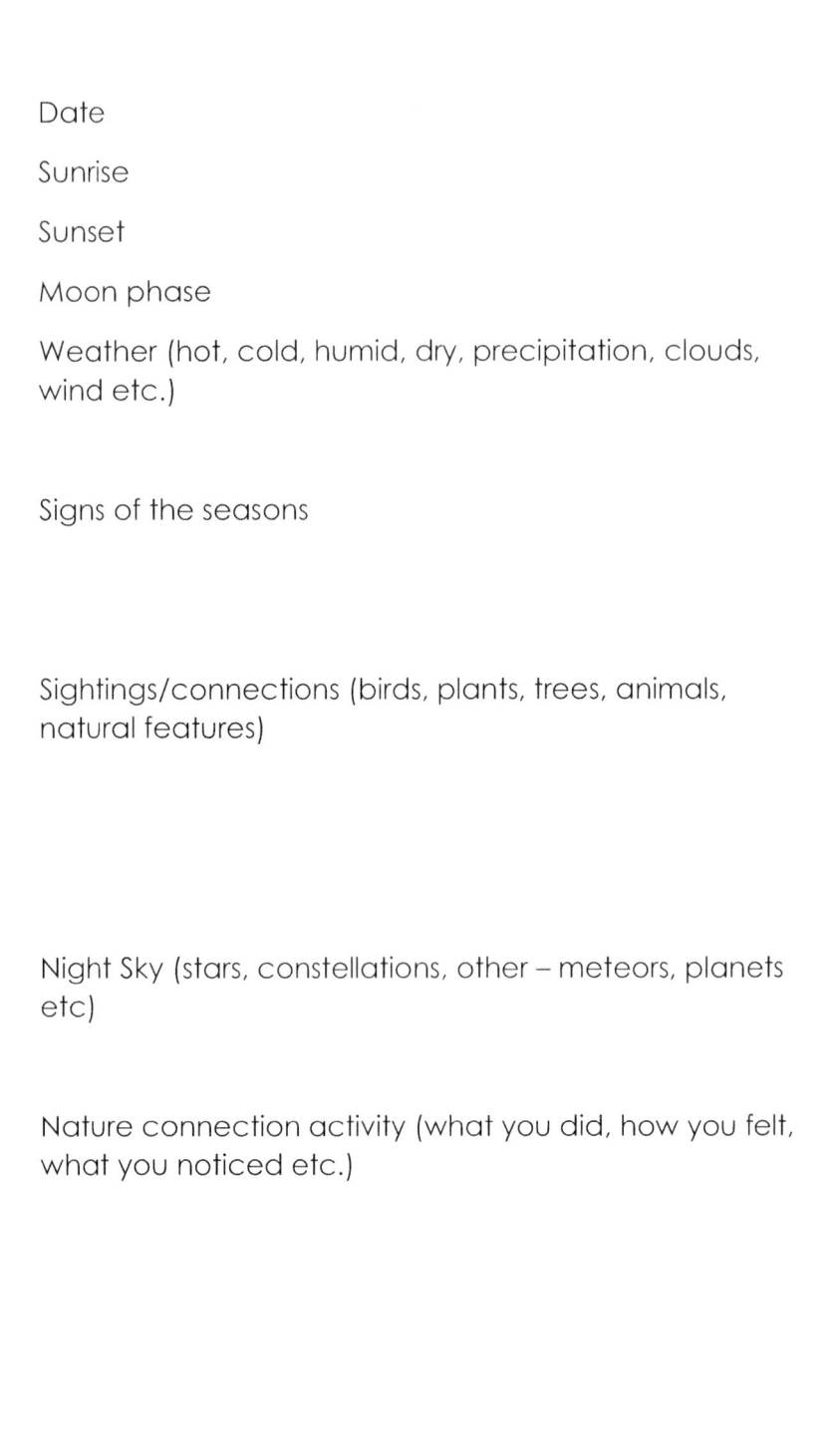

Drawings, pictures, stories, poems, extra notes, gratitudes, ways I gave service to nature

Date

Sunrise

Sunset

Moon phase

Weather (hot, cold, humid, dry, precipitation, clouds, wind etc.)

Signs of the seasons

Sightings/connections (birds, plants, trees, animals, natural features)

Night Sky (stars, constellations, other – meteors, planets etc)

Nature connection activity (what you did, how you felt, what you noticed etc.)

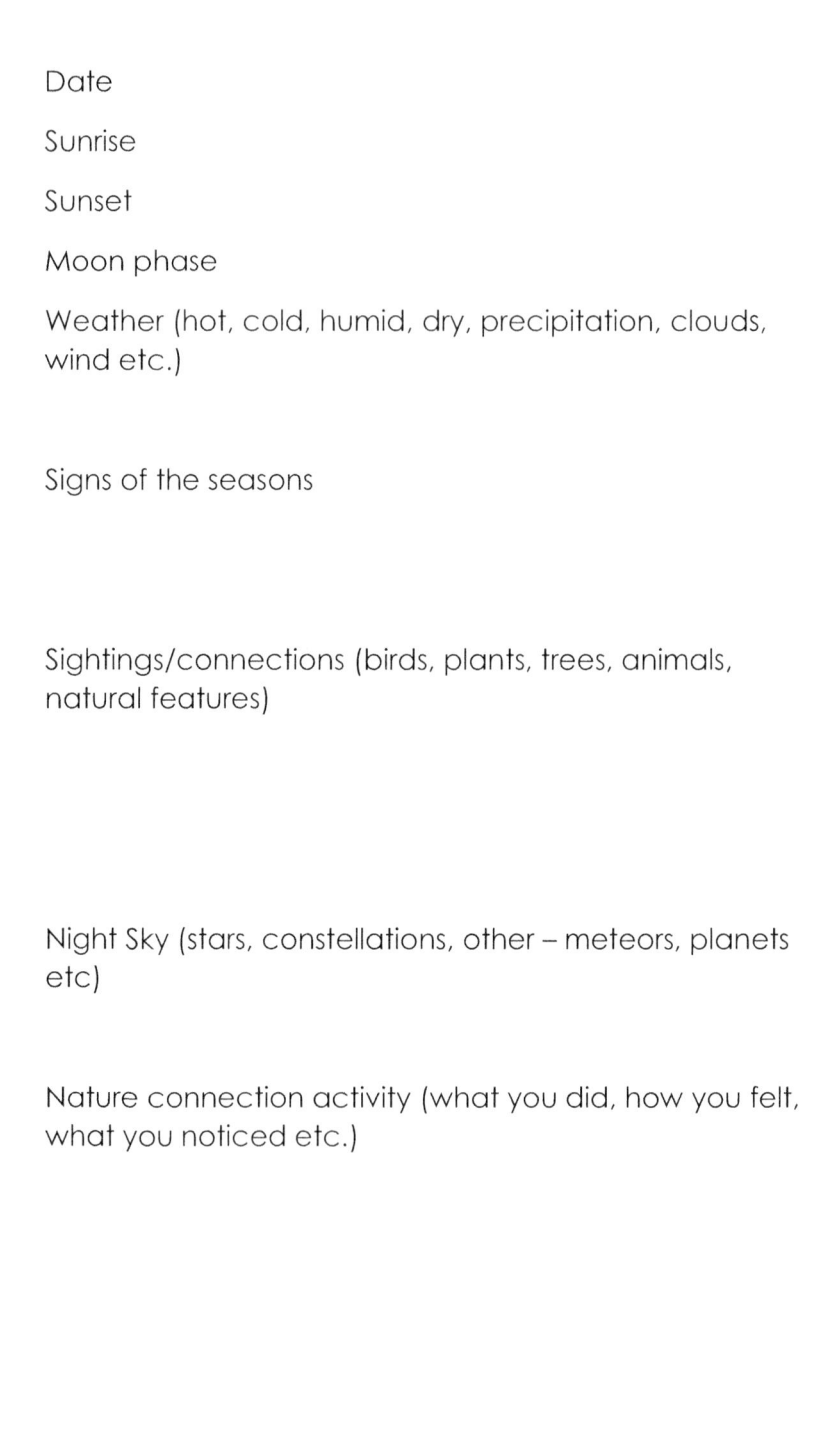

Drawings, pictures, stories, poems, extra notes, gratitudes, ways I gave service to nature

Date

Sunrise

Sunset

Moon phase

Weather (hot, cold, humid, dry, precipitation, clouds, wind etc.)

Signs of the seasons

Sightings/connections (birds, plants, trees, animals, natural features)

Night Sky (stars, constellations, other – meteors, planets etc)

Nature connection activity (what you did, how you felt, what you noticed etc.)

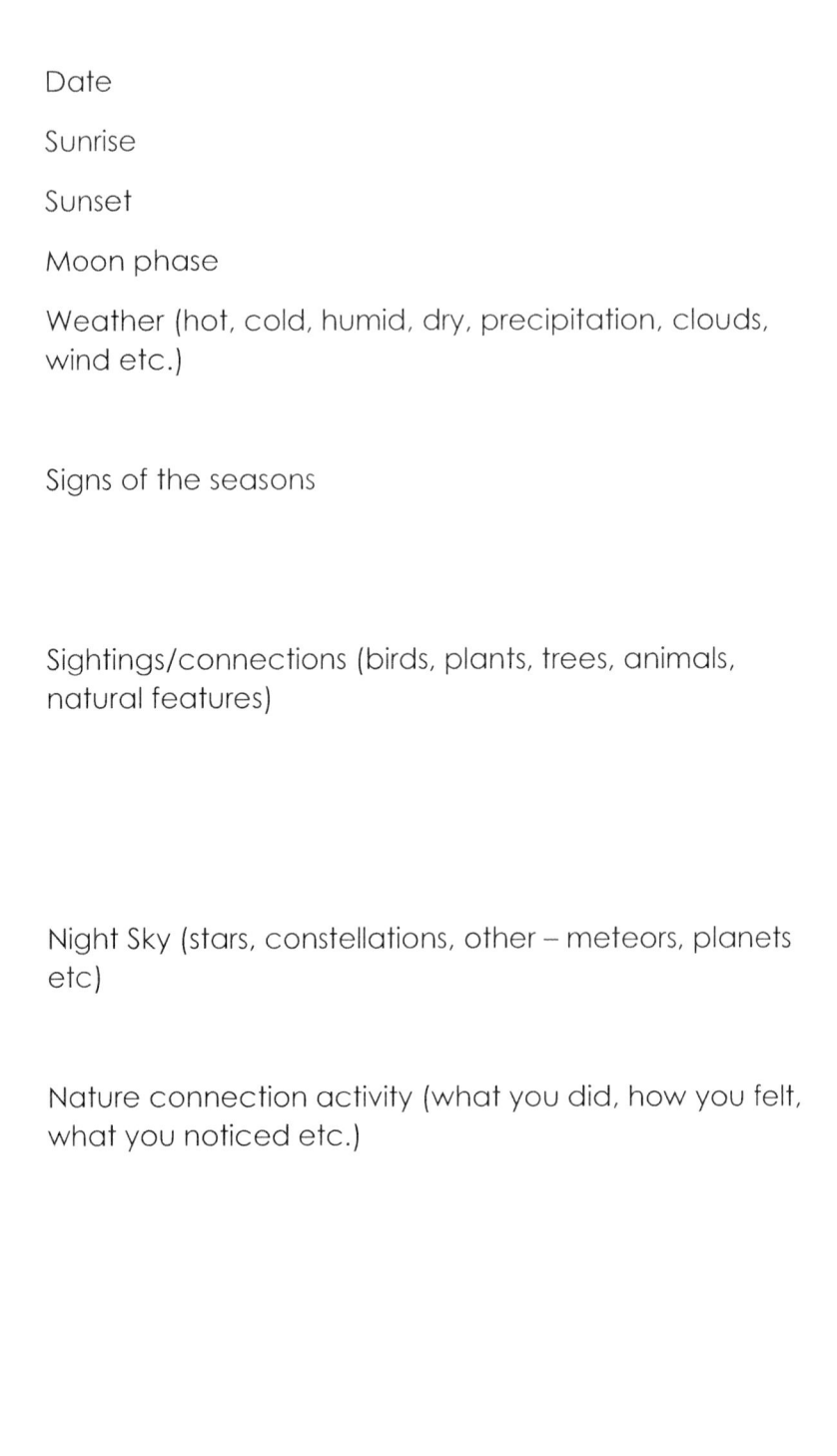

Drawings, pictures, stories, poems, extra notes, gratitudes, ways I gave service to nature

Date

Sunrise

Sunset

Moon phase

Weather (hot, cold, humid, dry, precipitation, clouds, wind etc.)

Signs of the seasons

Sightings/connections (birds, plants, trees, animals, natural features)

Night Sky (stars, constellations, other – meteors, planets etc)

Nature connection activity (what you did, how you felt, what you noticed etc.)

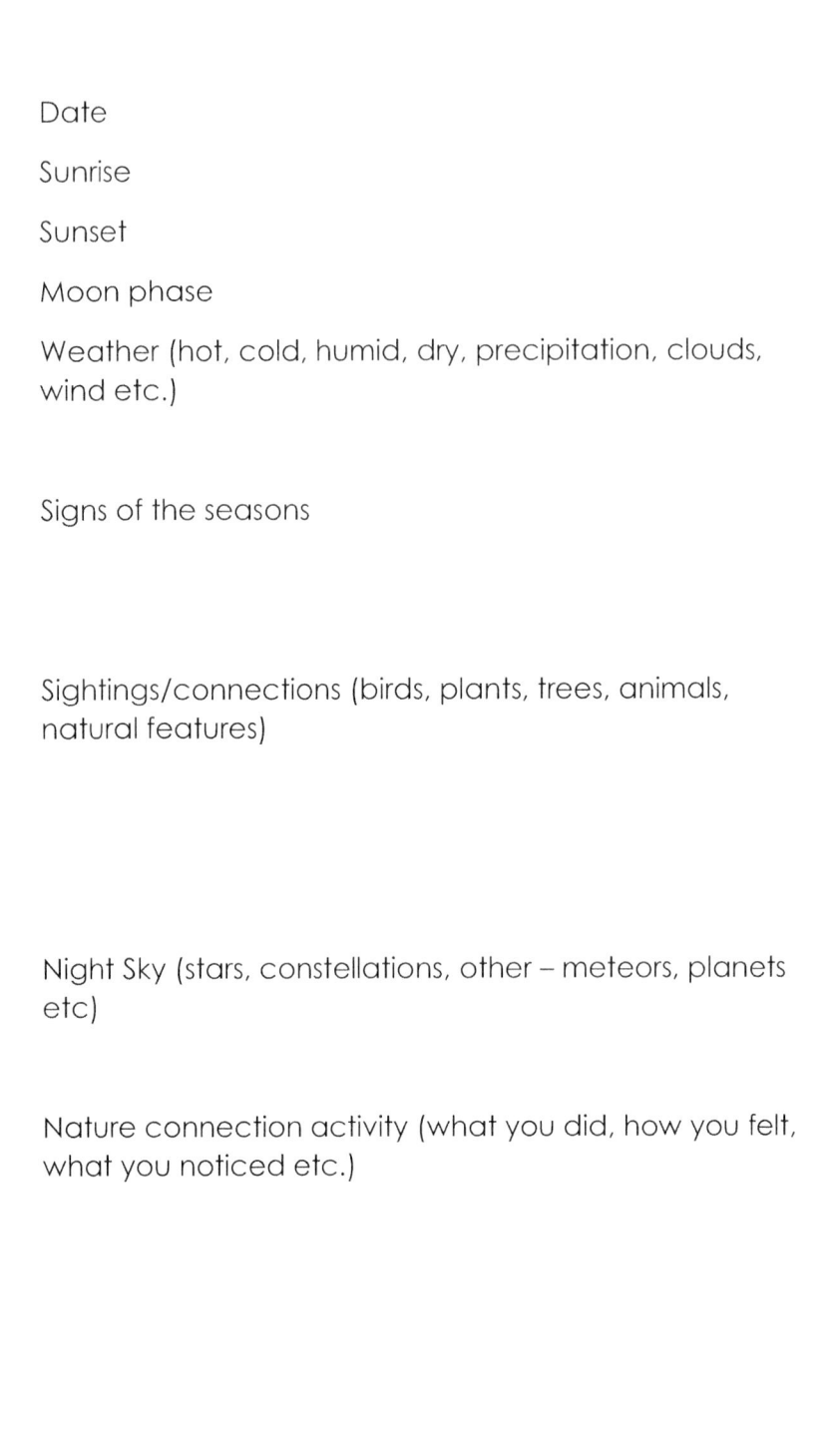

Drawings, pictures, stories, poems, extra notes, gratitudes, ways I gave service to nature

Date

Sunrise

Sunset

Moon phase

Weather (hot, cold, humid, dry, precipitation, clouds, wind etc.)

Signs of the seasons

Sightings/connections (birds, plants, trees, animals, natural features)

Night Sky (stars, constellations, other – meteors, planets etc)

Nature connection activity (what you did, how you felt, what you noticed etc.)

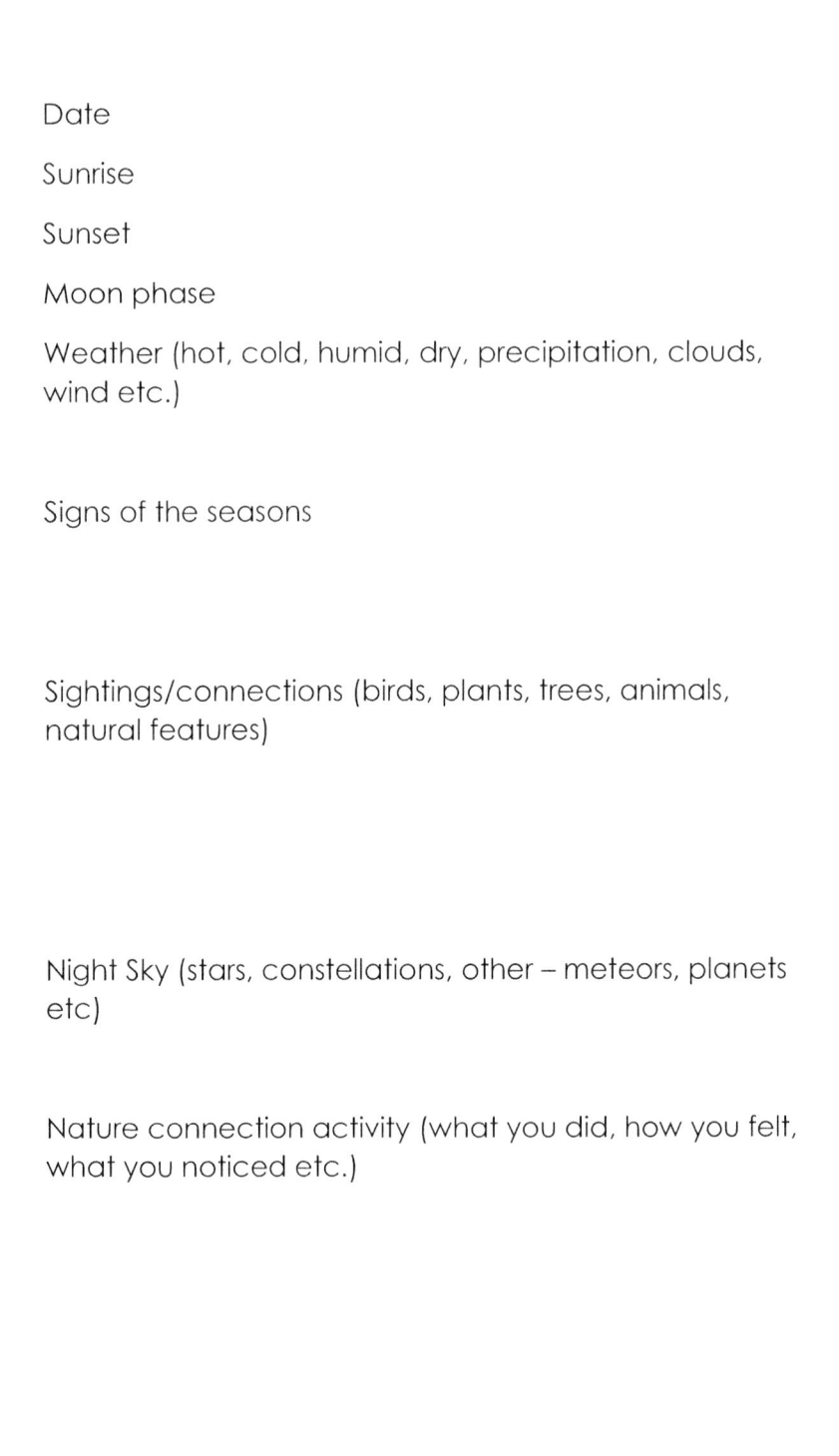

Drawings, pictures, stories, poems, extra notes, gratitudes, ways I gave service to nature

Date

Sunrise

Sunset

Moon phase

Weather (hot, cold, humid, dry, precipitation, clouds, wind etc.)

Signs of the seasons

Sightings/connections (birds, plants, trees, animals, natural features)

Night Sky (stars, constellations, other – meteors, planets etc)

Nature connection activity (what you did, how you felt, what you noticed etc.)

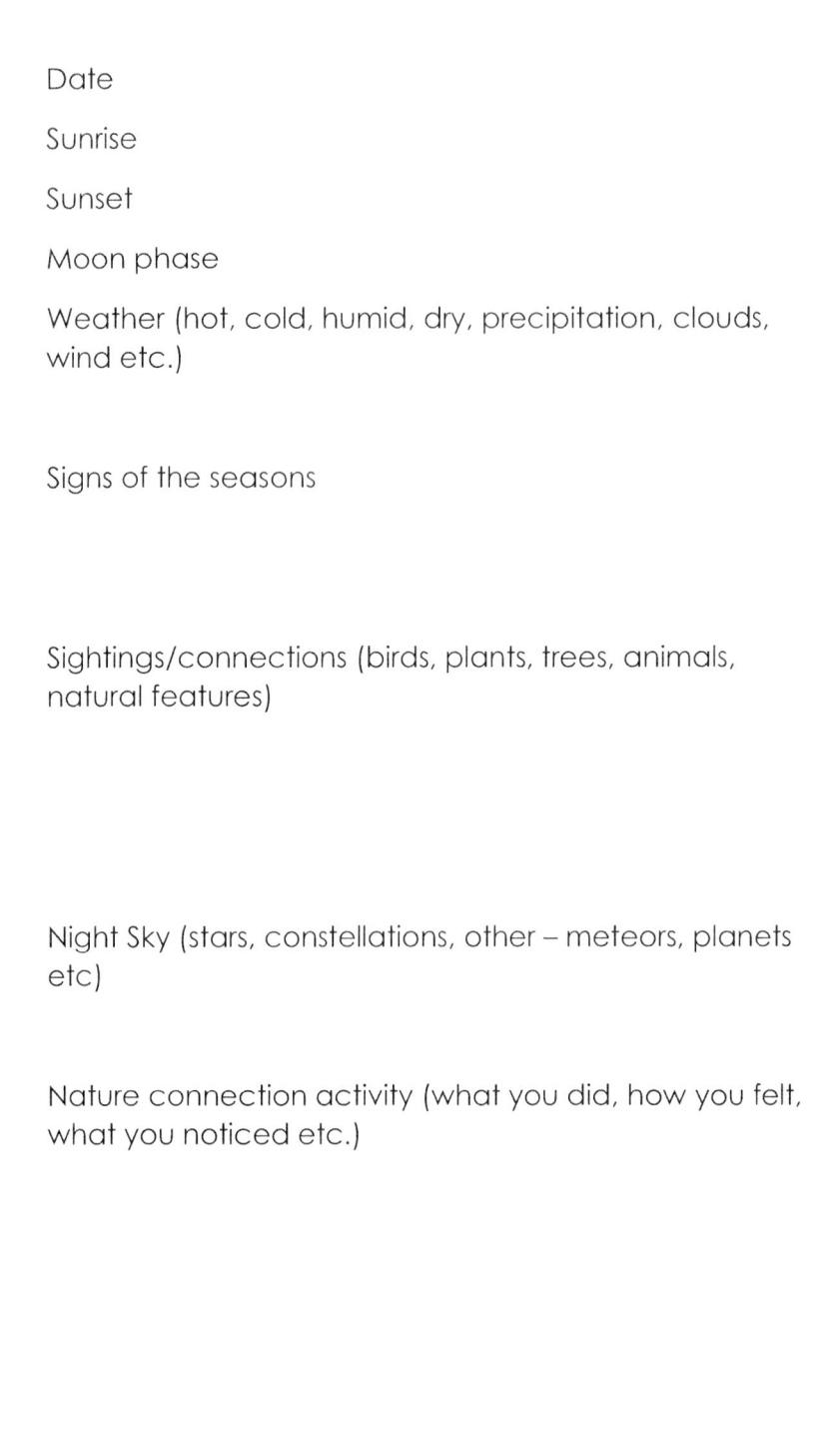

Drawings, pictures, stories, poems, extra notes, gratitudes, ways I gave service to nature

Date

Sunrise

Sunset

Moon phase

Weather (hot, cold, humid, dry, precipitation, clouds, wind etc.)

Signs of the seasons

Sightings/connections (birds, plants, trees, animals, natural features)

Night Sky (stars, constellations, other – meteors, planets etc)

Nature connection activity (what you did, how you felt, what you noticed etc.)

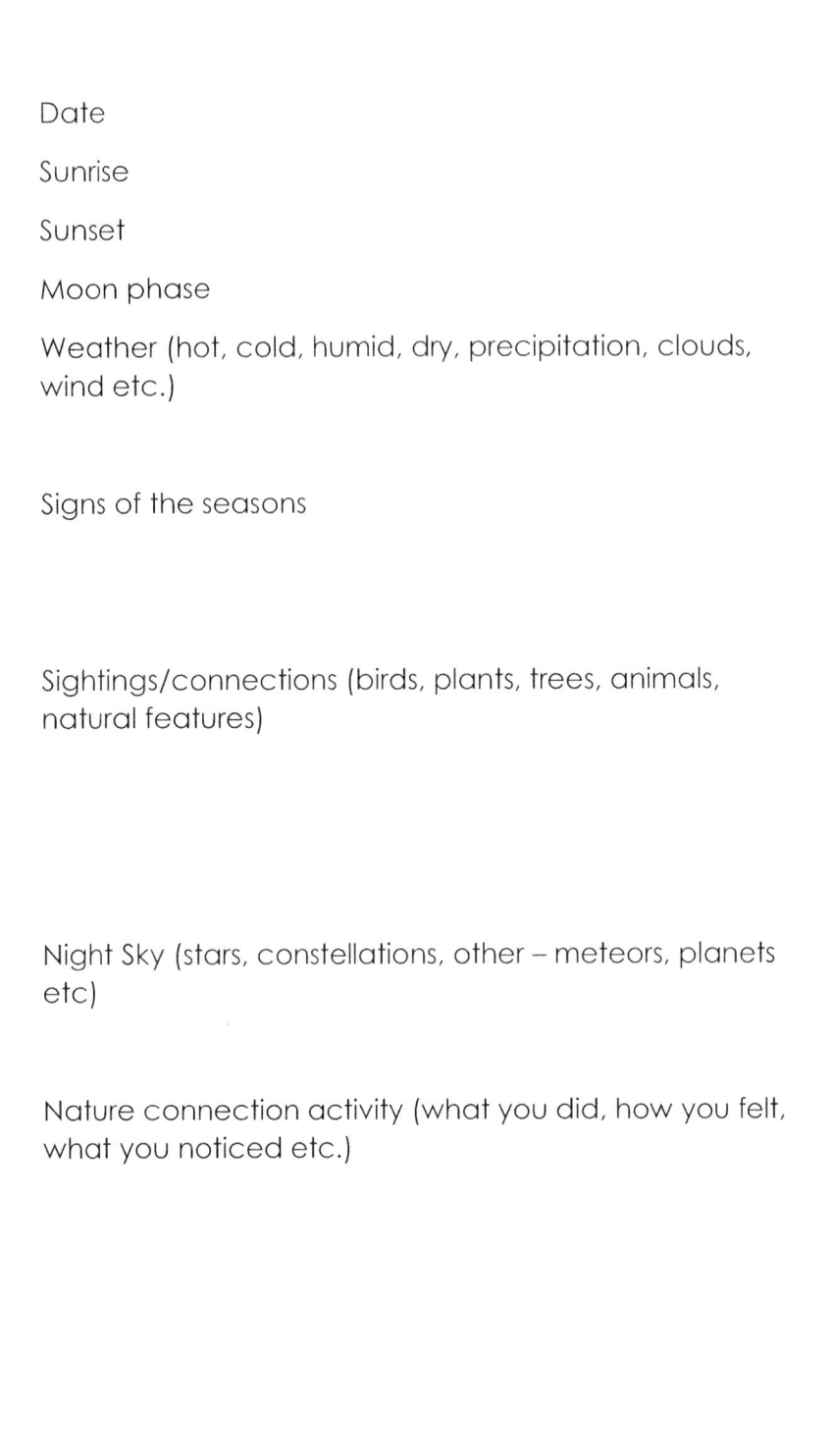

Drawings, pictures, stories, poems, extra notes, gratitudes, ways I gave service to nature

Date

Sunrise

Sunset

Moon phase

Weather (hot, cold, humid, dry, precipitation, clouds, wind etc.)

Signs of the seasons

Sightings/connections (birds, plants, trees, animals, natural features)

Night Sky (stars, constellations, other – meteors, planets etc)

Nature connection activity (what you did, how you felt, what you noticed etc.)

Drawings, pictures, stories, poems, extra notes, gratitudes, ways I gave service to nature

Date

Sunrise

Sunset

Moon phase

Weather (hot, cold, humid, dry, precipitation, clouds, wind etc.)

Signs of the seasons

Sightings/connections (birds, plants, trees, animals, natural features)

Night Sky (stars, constellations, other – meteors, planets etc)

Nature connection activity (what you did, how you felt, what you noticed etc.)

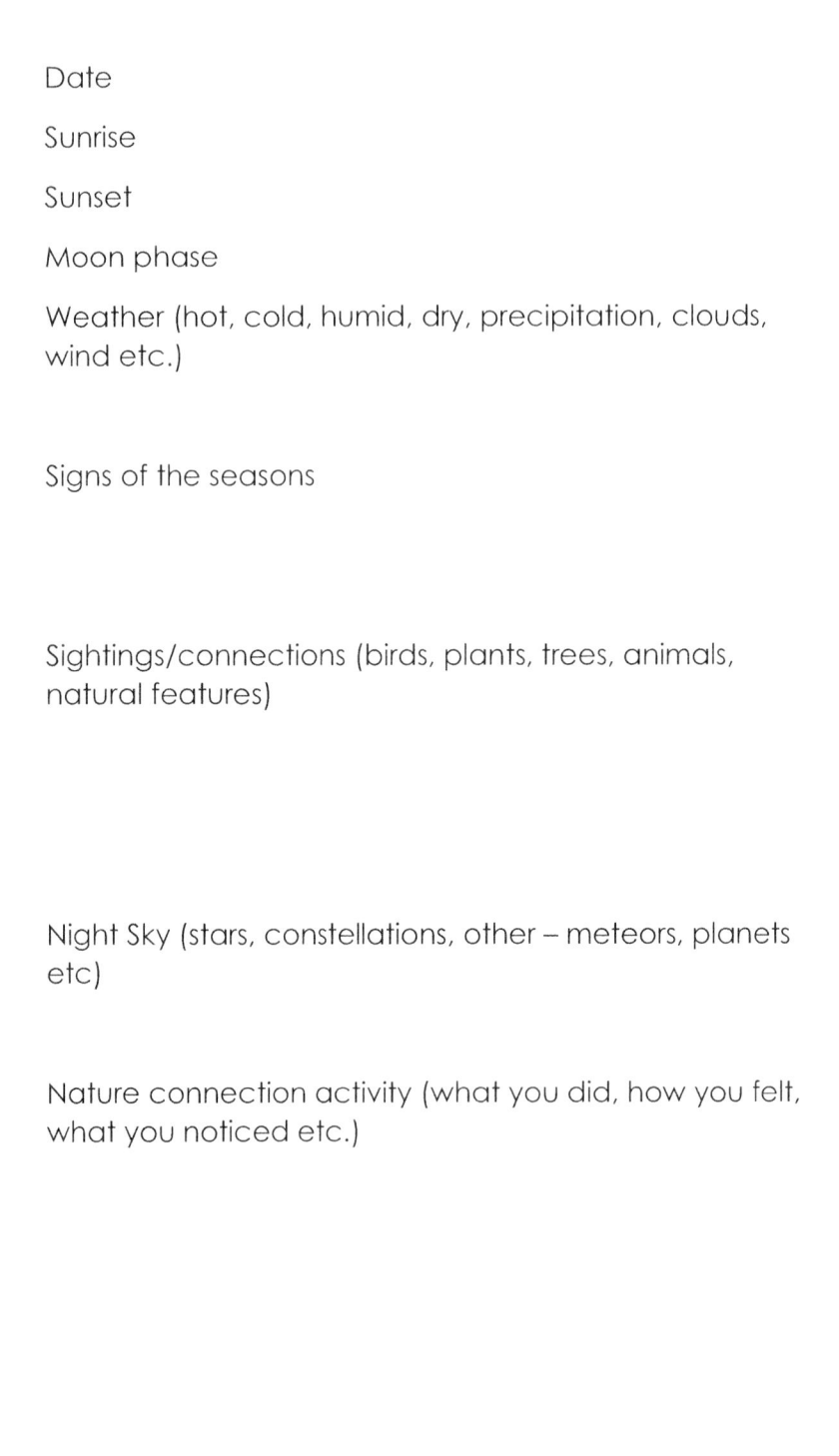

Drawings, pictures, stories, poems, extra notes, gratitudes, ways I gave service to nature

Date

Sunrise

Sunset

Moon phase

Weather (hot, cold, humid, dry, precipitation, clouds, wind etc.)

Signs of the seasons

Sightings/connections (birds, plants, trees, animals, natural features)

Night Sky (stars, constellations, other – meteors, planets etc)

Nature connection activity (what you did, how you felt, what you noticed etc.)

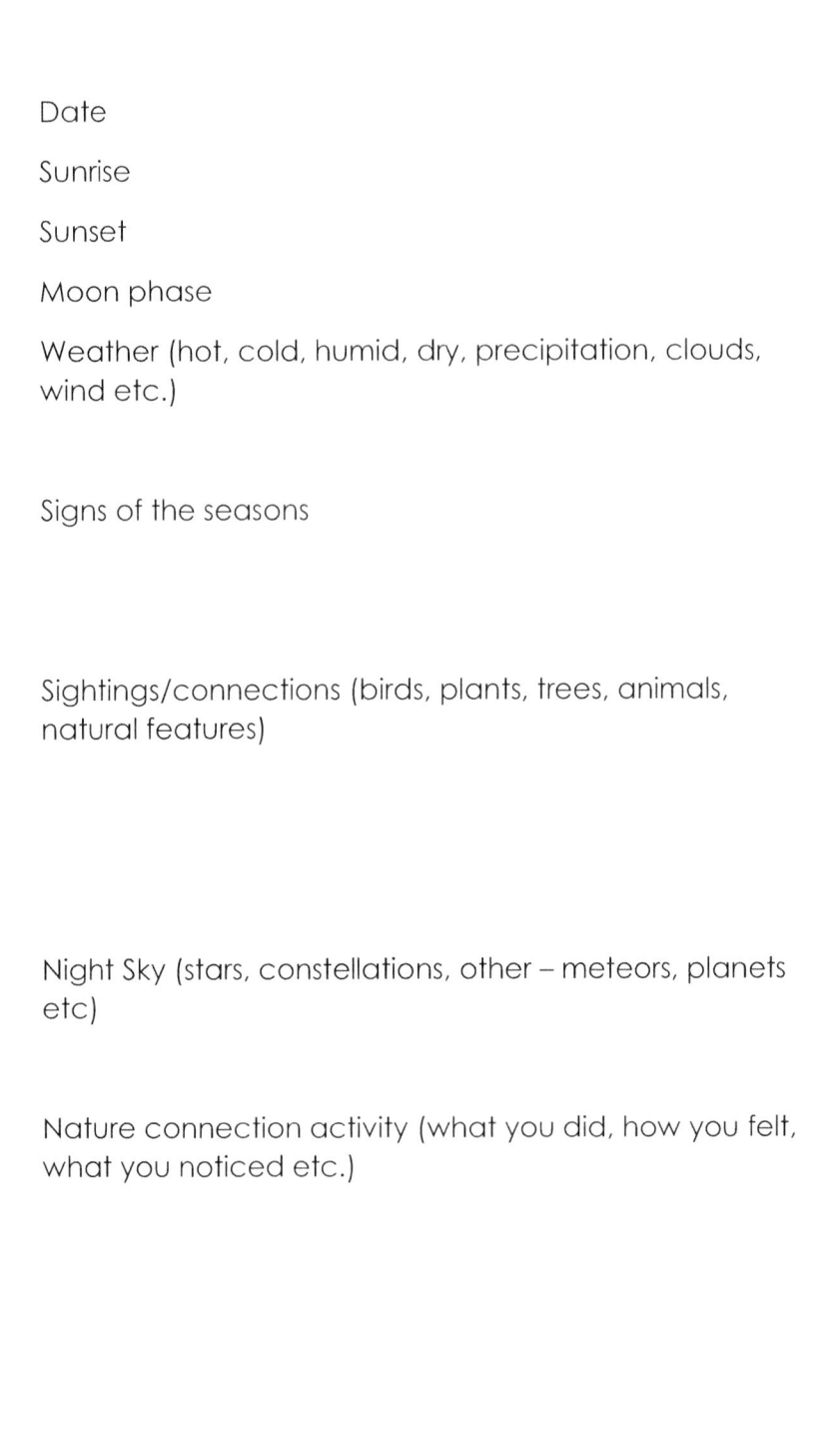

Drawings, pictures, stories, poems, extra notes, gratitudes, ways I gave service to nature

Date

Sunrise

Sunset

Moon phase

Weather (hot, cold, humid, dry, precipitation, clouds, wind etc.)

Signs of the seasons

Sightings/connections (birds, plants, trees, animals, natural features)

Night Sky (stars, constellations, other – meteors, planets etc)

Nature connection activity (what you did, how you felt, what you noticed etc.)

Drawings, pictures, stories, poems, extra notes, gratitudes, ways I gave service to nature

Date

Sunrise

Sunset

Moon phase

Weather (hot, cold, humid, dry, precipitation, clouds, wind etc.)

Signs of the seasons

Sightings/connections (birds, plants, trees, animals, natural features)

Night Sky (stars, constellations, other – meteors, planets etc)

Nature connection activity (what you did, how you felt, what you noticed etc.)

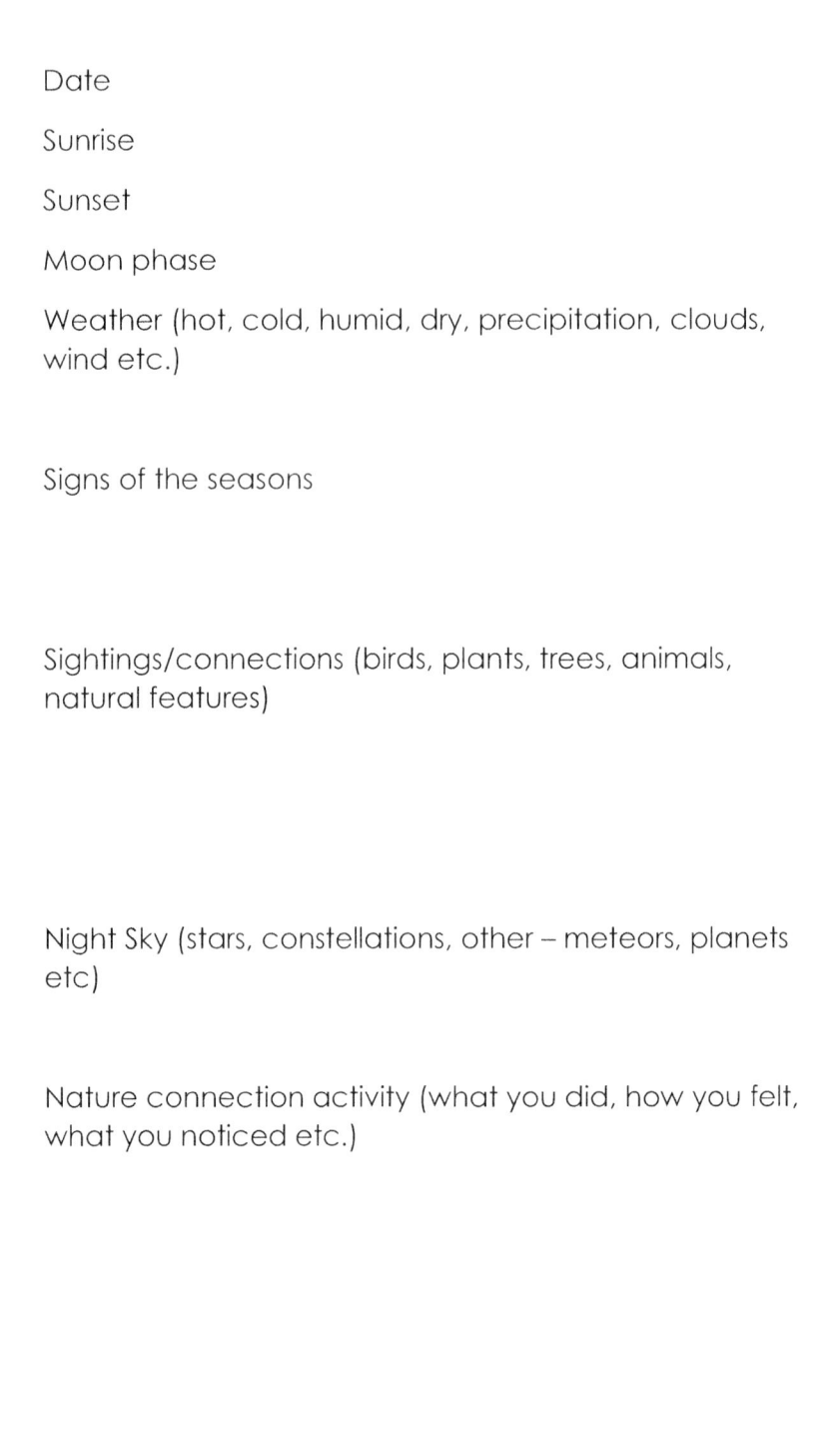

Drawings, pictures, stories, poems, extra notes, gratitudes, ways I gave service to nature

Date

Sunrise

Sunset

Moon phase

Weather (hot, cold, humid, dry, precipitation, clouds, wind etc.)

Signs of the seasons

Sightings/connections (birds, plants, trees, animals, natural features)

Night Sky (stars, constellations, other – meteors, planets etc)

Nature connection activity (what you did, how you felt, what you noticed etc.)

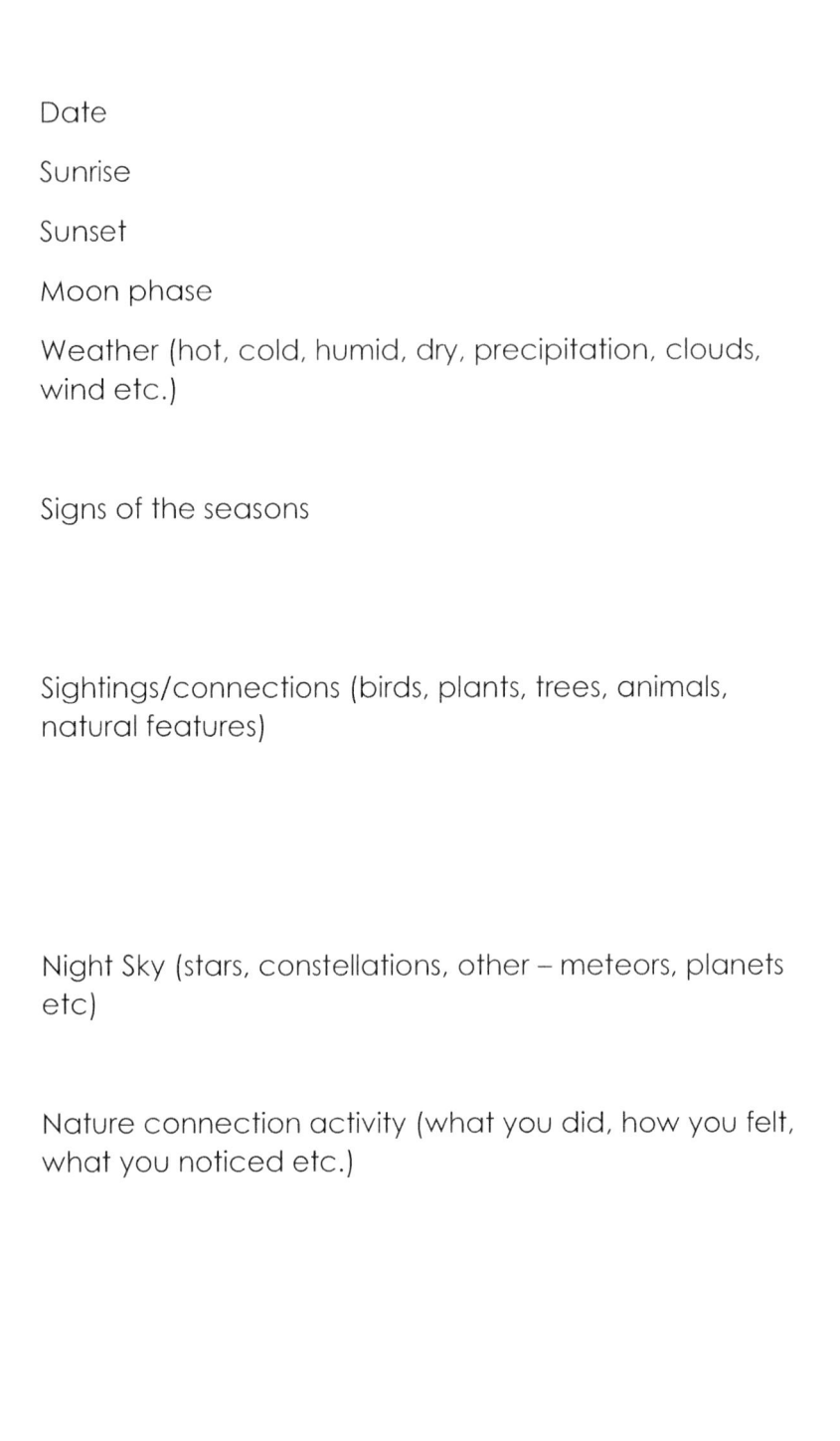

Drawings, pictures, stories, poems, extra notes, gratitudes, ways I gave service to nature

Date

Sunrise

Sunset

Moon phase

Weather (hot, cold, humid, dry, precipitation, clouds, wind etc.)

Signs of the seasons

Sightings/connections (birds, plants, trees, animals, natural features)

Night Sky (stars, constellations, other – meteors, planets etc)

Nature connection activity (what you did, how you felt, what you noticed etc.)

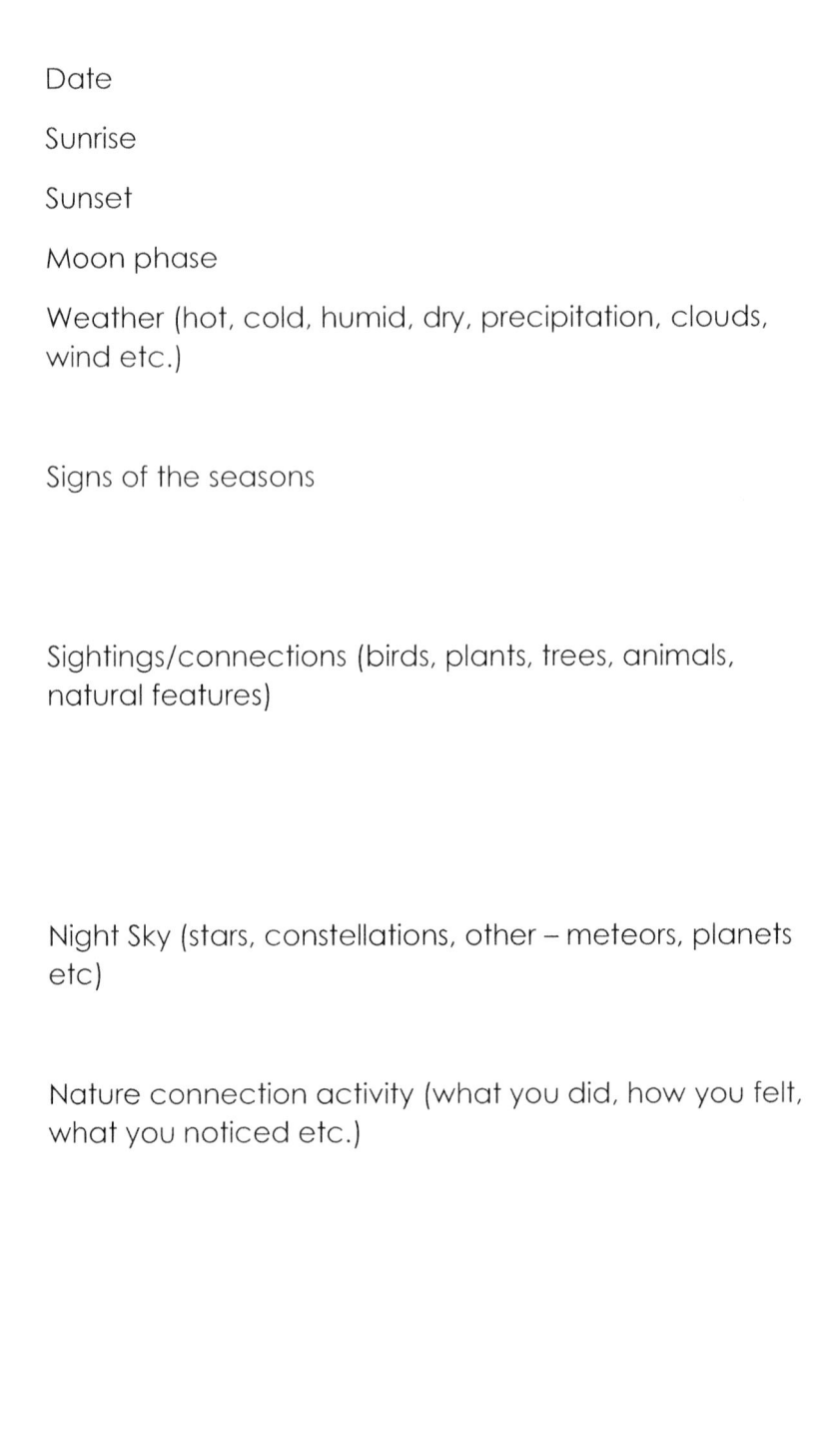

Drawings, pictures, stories, poems, extra notes, gratitudes, ways I gave service to nature

Date

Sunrise

Sunset

Moon phase

Weather (hot, cold, humid, dry, precipitation, clouds, wind etc.)

Signs of the seasons

Sightings/connections (birds, plants, trees, animals, natural features)

Night Sky (stars, constellations, other – meteors, planets etc)

Nature connection activity (what you did, how you felt, what you noticed etc.)

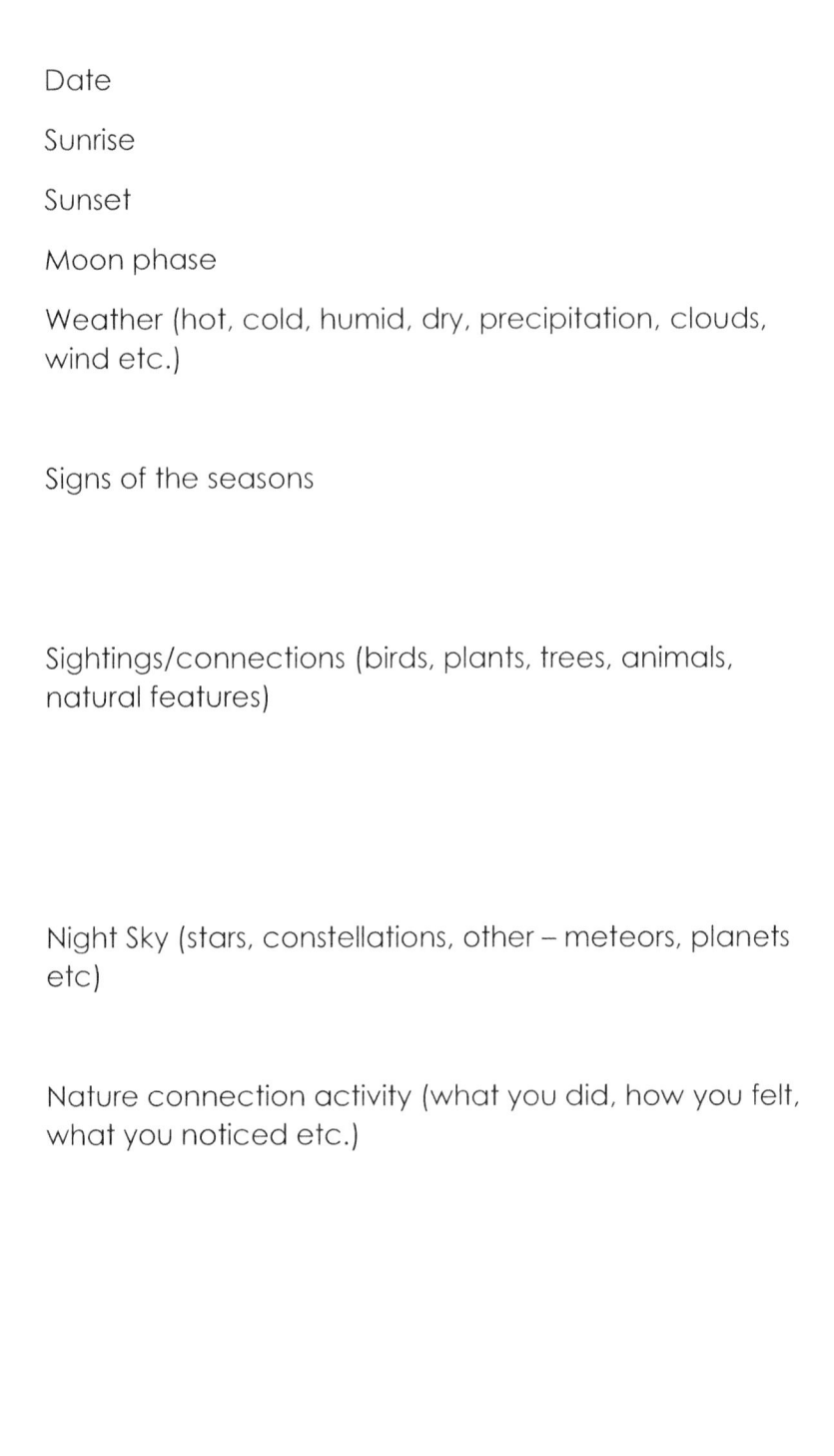

Drawings, pictures, stories, poems, extra notes, gratitudes, ways I gave service to nature

Date

Sunrise

Sunset

Moon phase

Weather (hot, cold, humid, dry, precipitation, clouds, wind etc.)

Signs of the seasons

Sightings/connections (birds, plants, trees, animals, natural features)

Night Sky (stars, constellations, other – meteors, planets etc)

Nature connection activity (what you did, how you felt, what you noticed etc.)

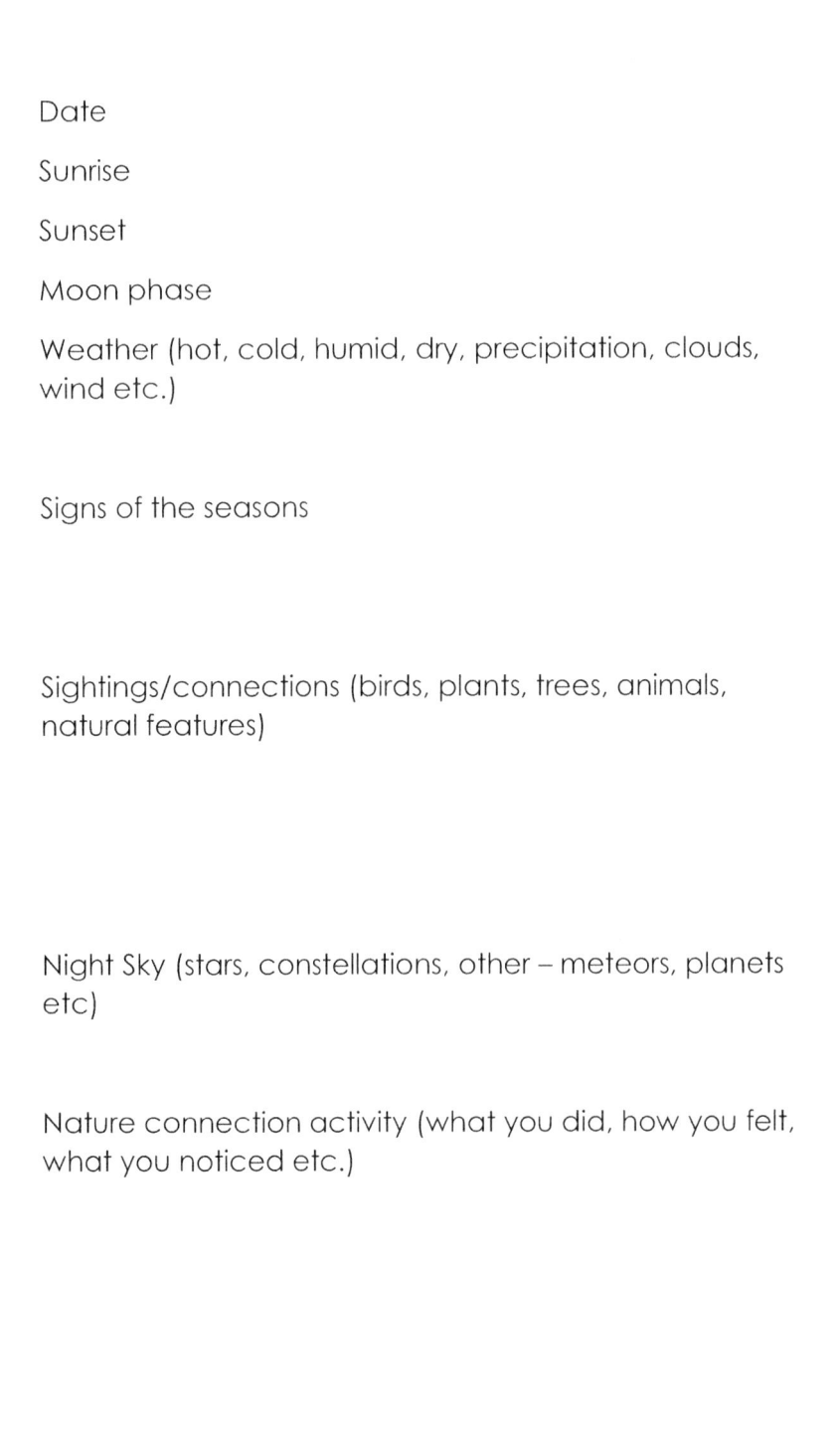

Drawings, pictures, stories, poems, extra notes, gratitudes, ways I gave service to nature

Date

Sunrise

Sunset

Moon phase

Weather (hot, cold, humid, dry, precipitation, clouds, wind etc.)

Signs of the seasons

Sightings/connections (birds, plants, trees, animals, natural features)

Night Sky (stars, constellations, other – meteors, planets etc)

Nature connection activity (what you did, how you felt, what you noticed etc.)

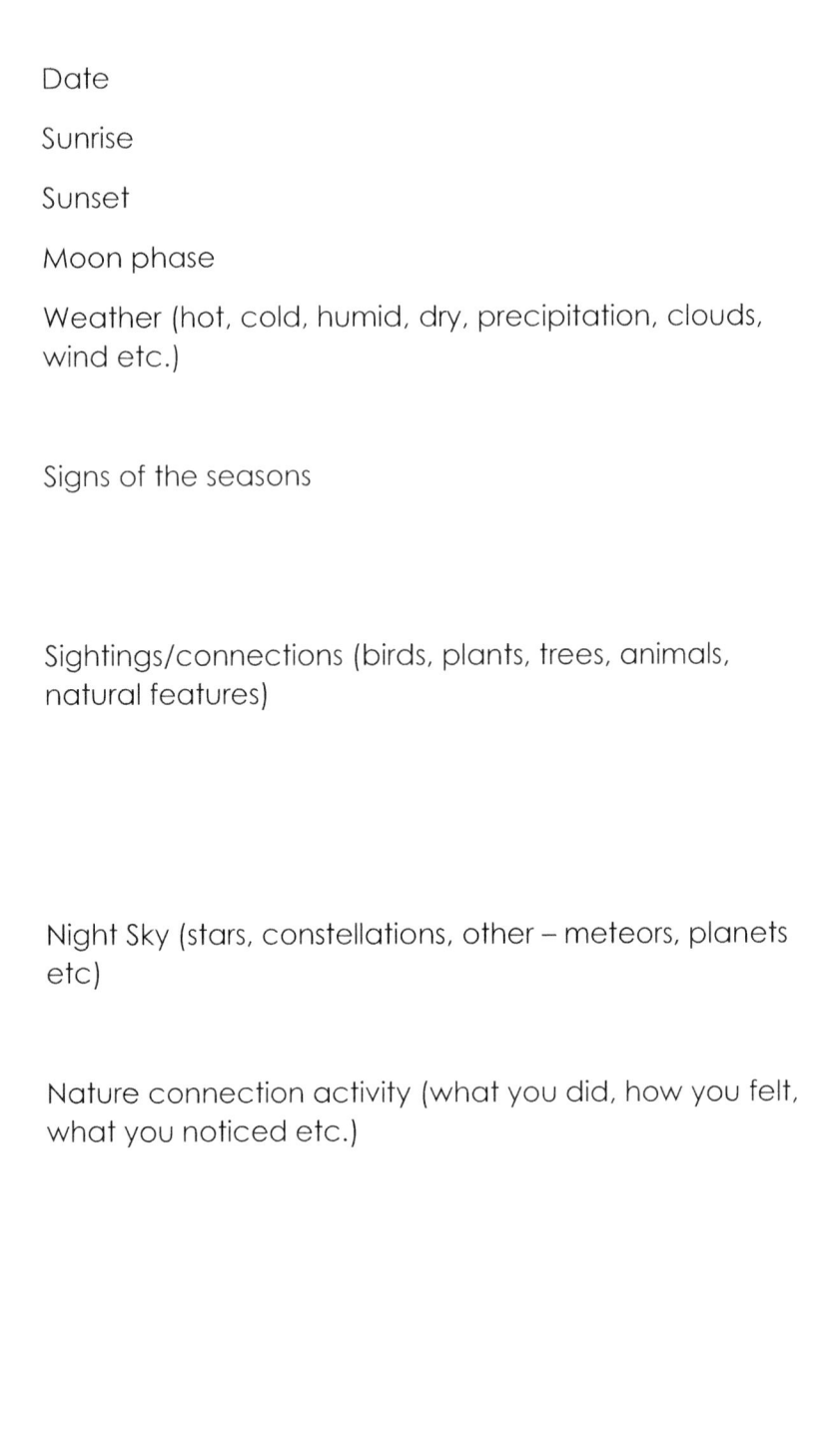

Drawings, pictures, stories, poems, extra notes, gratitudes, ways I gave service to nature

Date

Sunrise

Sunset

Moon phase

Weather (hot, cold, humid, dry, precipitation, clouds, wind etc.)

Signs of the seasons

Sightings/connections (birds, plants, trees, animals, natural features)

Night Sky (stars, constellations, other – meteors, planets etc)

Nature connection activity (what you did, how you felt, what you noticed etc.)

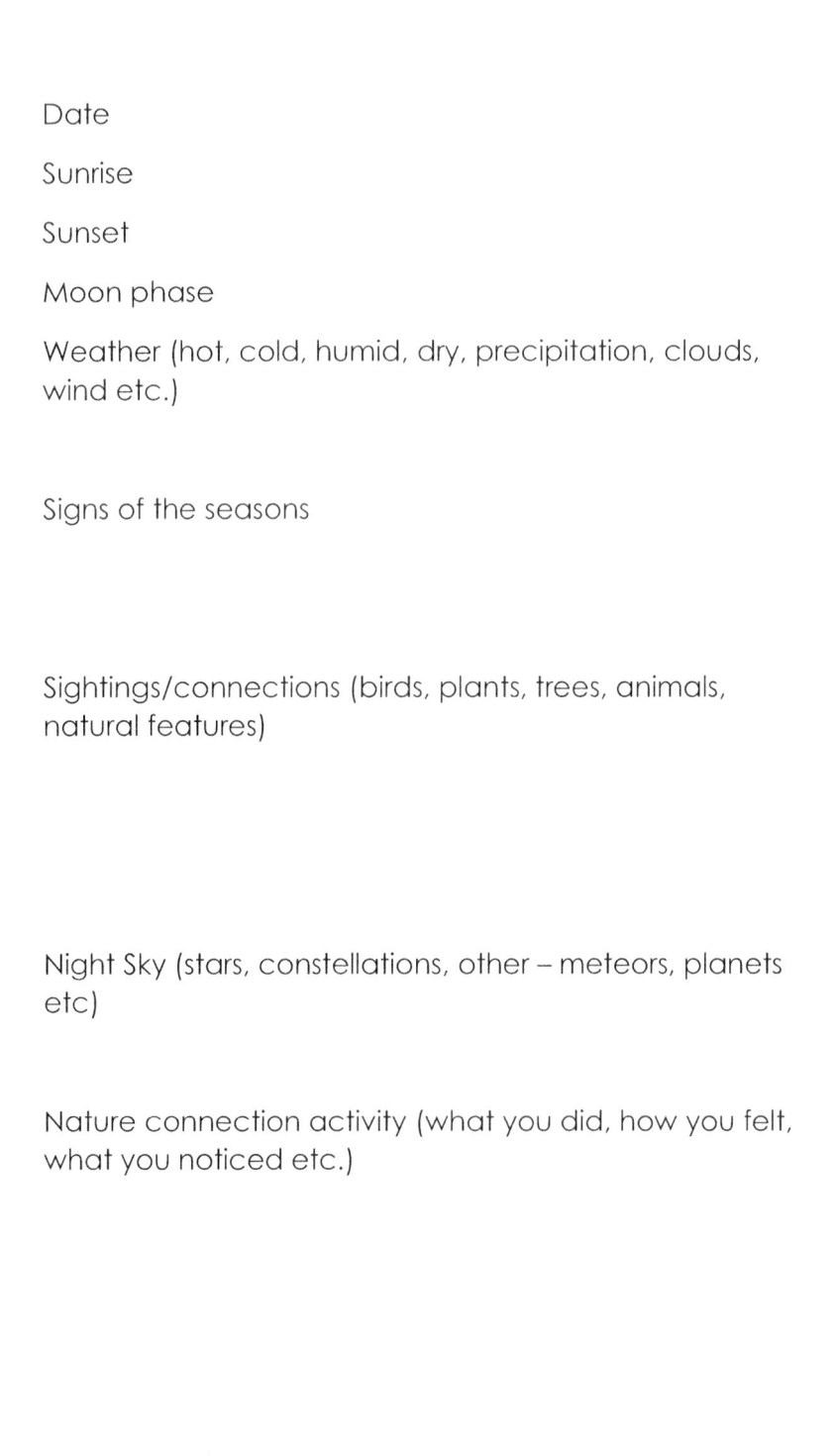

Drawings, pictures, stories, poems, extra notes, gratitudes, ways I gave service to nature

Date

Sunrise

Sunset

Moon phase

Weather (hot, cold, humid, dry, precipitation, clouds, wind etc.)

Signs of the seasons

Sightings/connections (birds, plants, trees, animals, natural features)

Night Sky (stars, constellations, other – meteors, planets etc)

Nature connection activity (what you did, how you felt, what you noticed etc.)

Drawings, pictures, stories, poems, extra notes, gratitudes, ways I gave service to nature

Date

Sunrise

Sunset

Moon phase

Weather (hot, cold, humid, dry, precipitation, clouds, wind etc.)

Signs of the seasons

Sightings/connections (birds, plants, trees, animals, natural features)

Night Sky (stars, constellations, other – meteors, planets etc)

Nature connection activity (what you did, how you felt, what you noticed etc.)

Drawings, pictures, stories, poems, extra notes, gratitudes, ways I gave service to nature

Date

Sunrise

Sunset

Moon phase

Weather (hot, cold, humid, dry, precipitation, clouds, wind etc.)

Signs of the seasons

Sightings/connections (birds, plants, trees, animals, natural features)

Night Sky (stars, constellations, other – meteors, planets etc)

Nature connection activity (what you did, how you felt, what you noticed etc.)

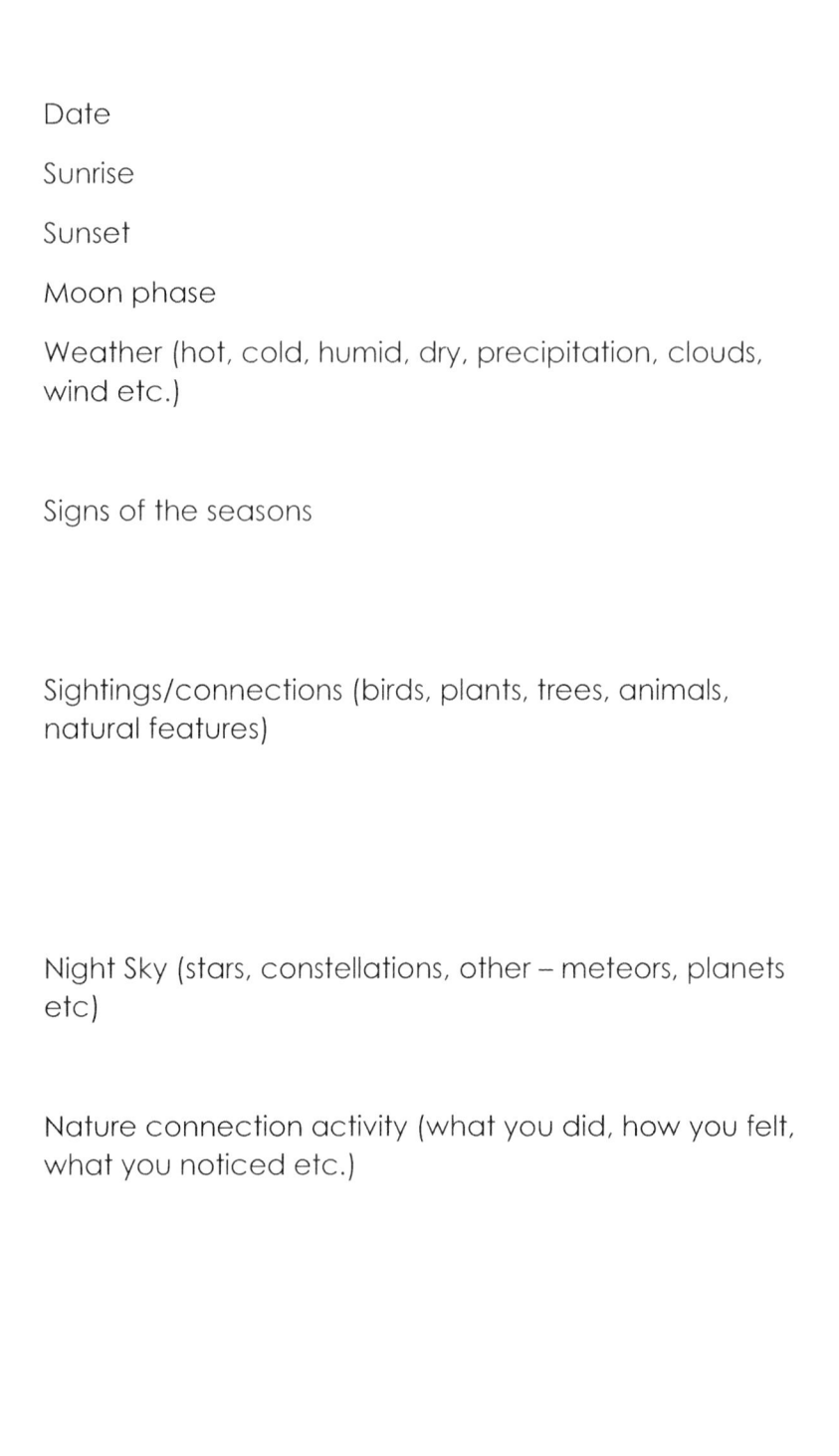

Drawings, pictures, stories, poems, extra notes, gratitudes, ways I gave service to nature

Date

Sunrise

Sunset

Moon phase

Weather (hot, cold, humid, dry, precipitation, clouds, wind etc.)

Signs of the seasons

Sightings/connections (birds, plants, trees, animals, natural features)

Night Sky (stars, constellations, other – meteors, planets etc)

Nature connection activity (what you did, how you felt, what you noticed etc.)

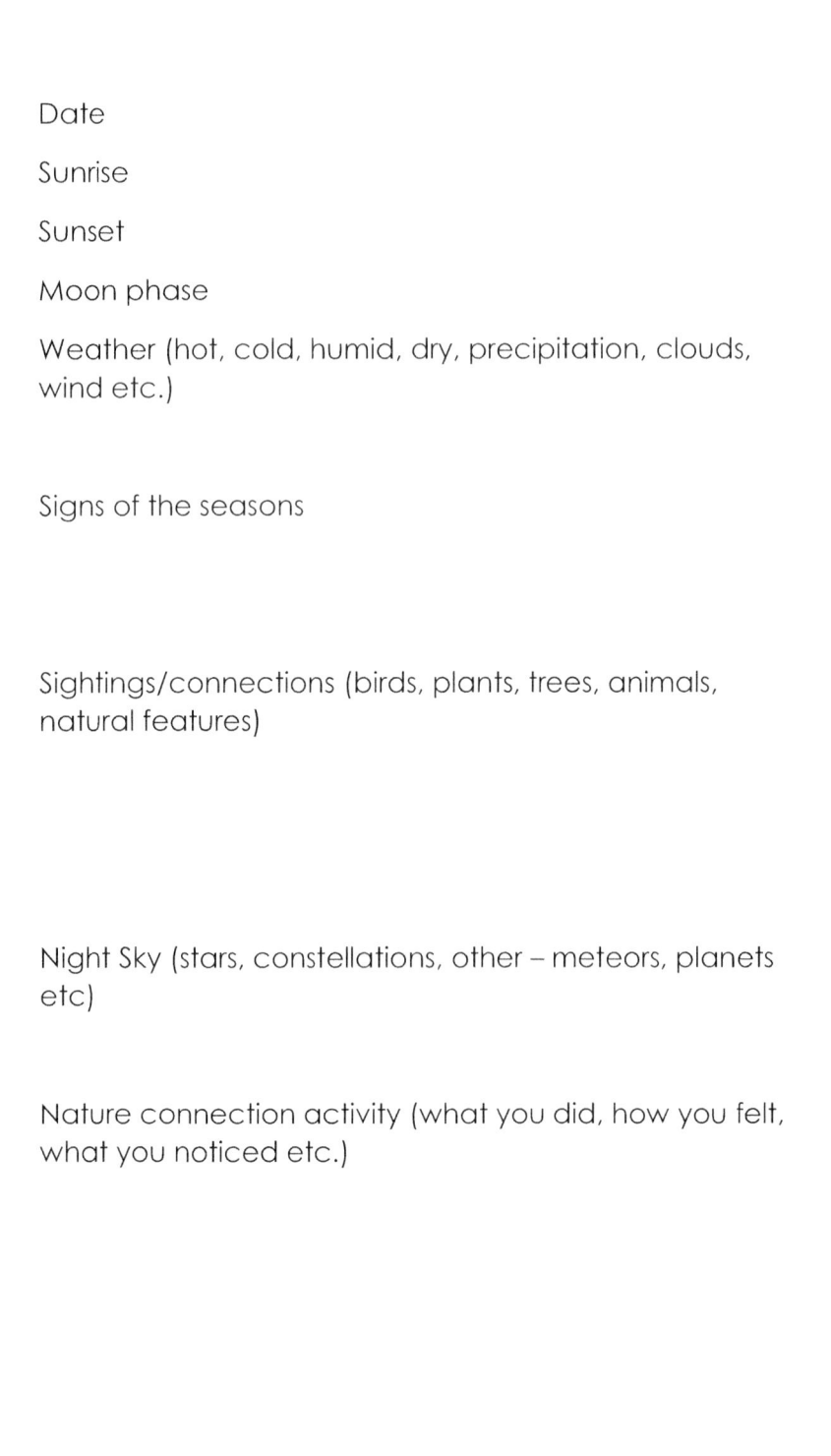

Drawings, pictures, stories, poems, extra notes, gratitudes, ways I gave service to nature

Date

Sunrise

Sunset

Moon phase

Weather (hot, cold, humid, dry, precipitation, clouds, wind etc.)

Signs of the seasons

Sightings/connections (birds, plants, trees, animals, natural features)

Night Sky (stars, constellations, other – meteors, planets etc)

Nature connection activity (what you did, how you felt, what you noticed etc.)

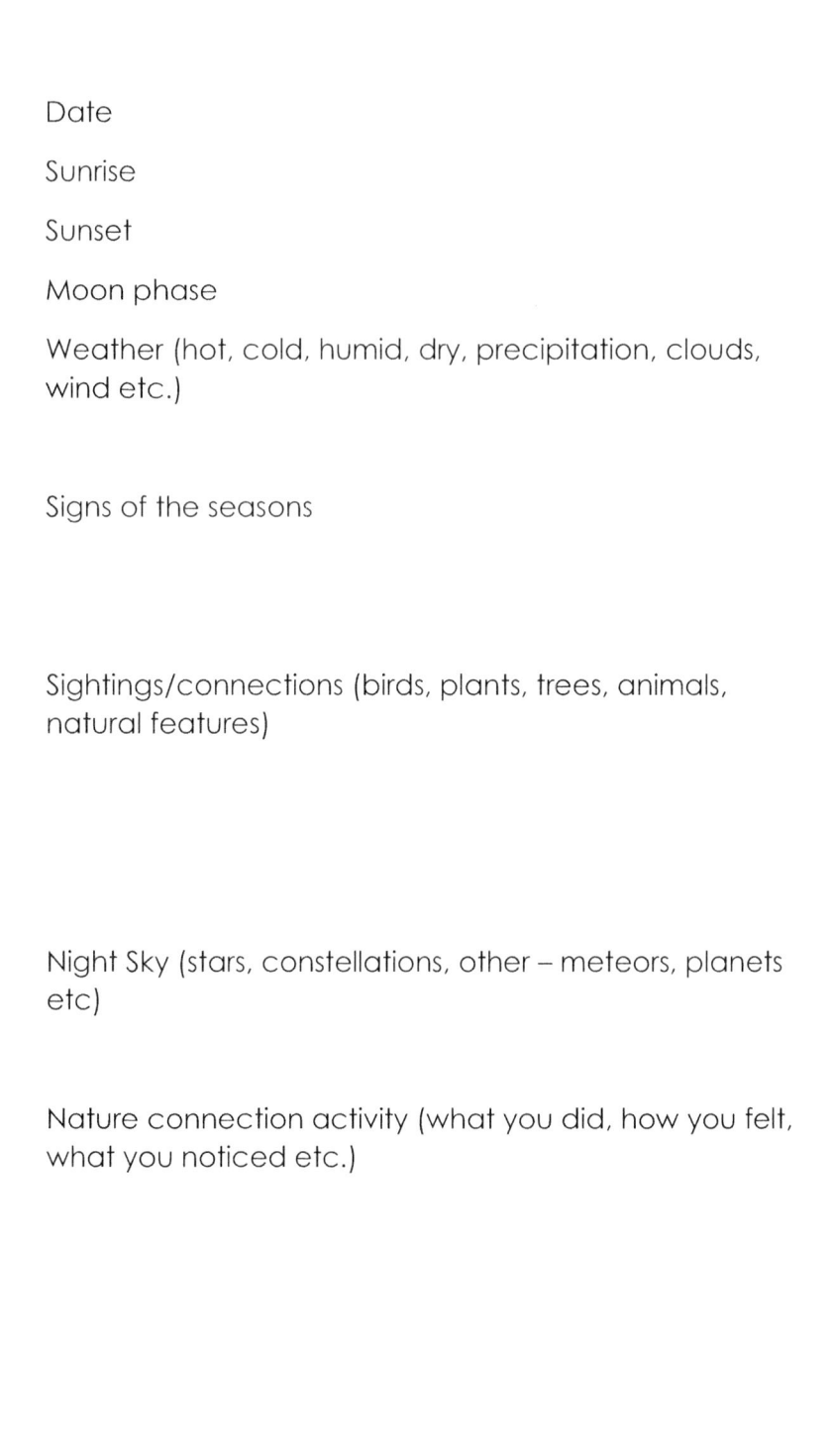

Drawings, pictures, stories, poems, extra notes, gratitudes, ways I gave service to nature

Date

Sunrise

Sunset

Moon phase

Weather (hot, cold, humid, dry, precipitation, clouds, wind etc.)

Signs of the seasons

Sightings/connections (birds, plants, trees, animals, natural features)

Night Sky (stars, constellations, other – meteors, planets etc)

Nature connection activity (what you did, how you felt, what you noticed etc.)

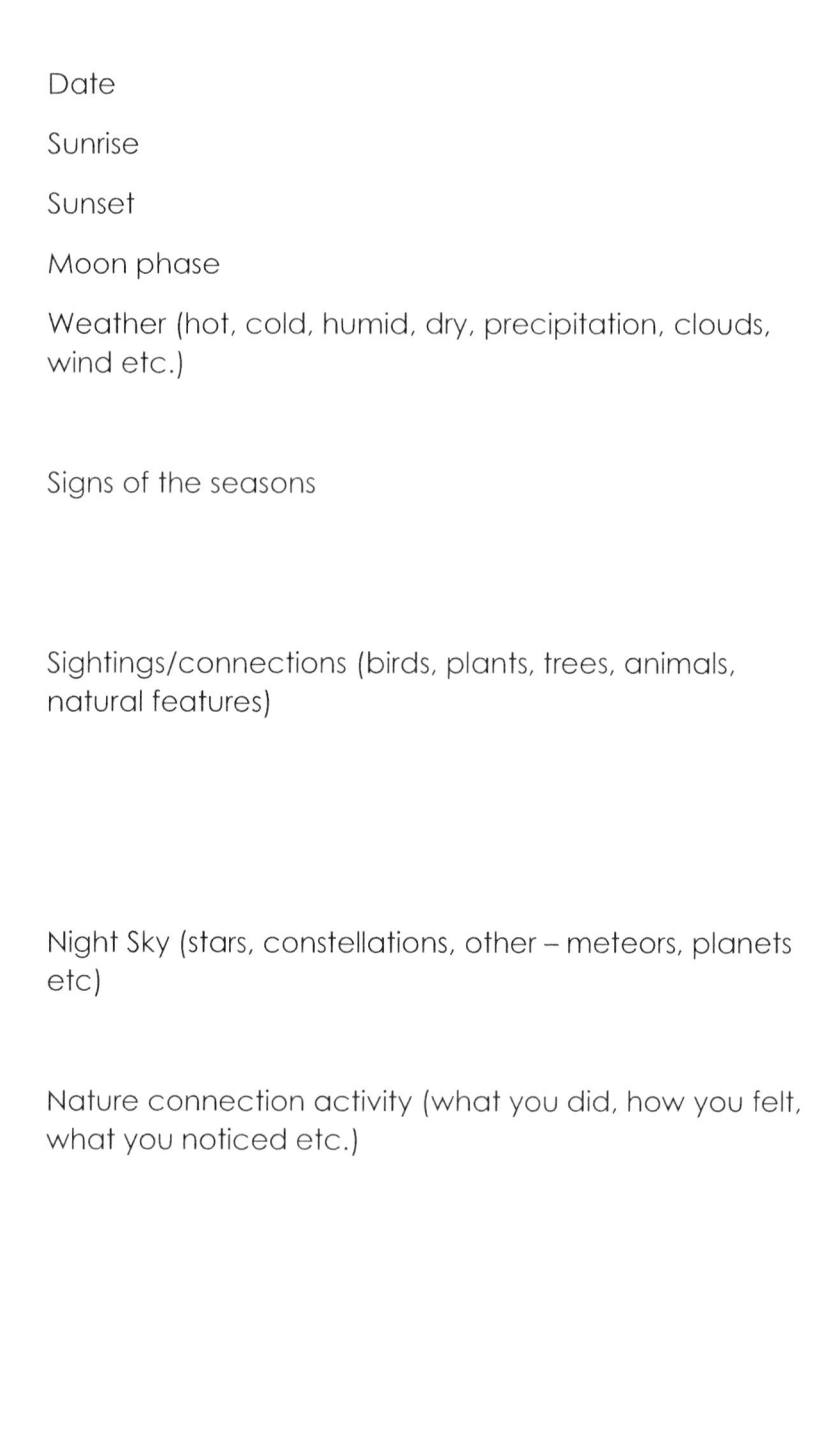

Drawings, pictures, stories, poems, extra notes, gratitudes, ways I gave service to nature

Date

Sunrise

Sunset

Moon phase

Weather (hot, cold, humid, dry, precipitation, clouds, wind etc.)

Signs of the seasons

Sightings/connections (birds, plants, trees, animals, natural features)

Night Sky (stars, constellations, other – meteors, planets etc)

Nature connection activity (what you did, how you felt, what you noticed etc.)

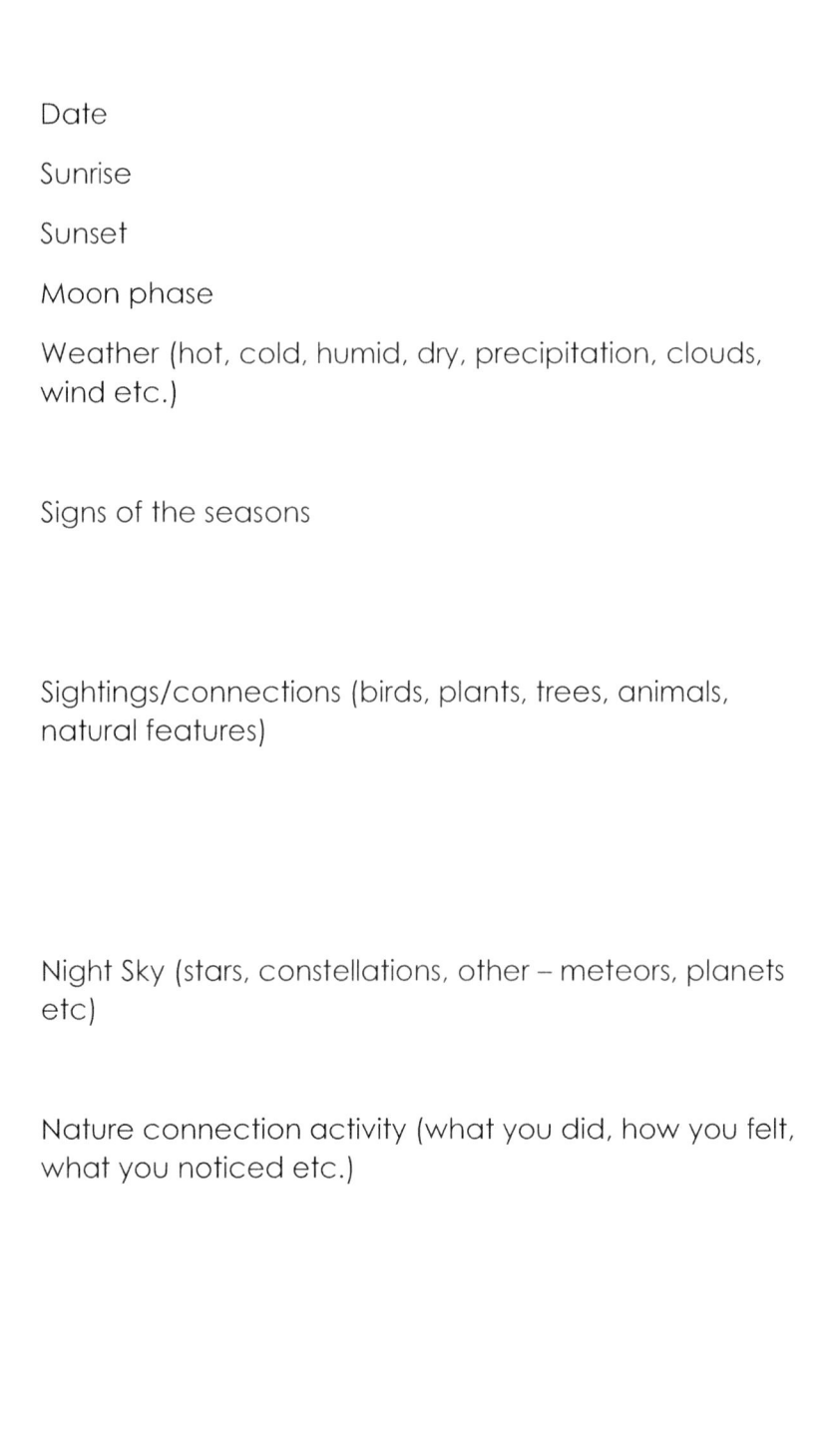

Drawings, pictures, stories, poems, extra notes, gratitudes, ways I gave service to nature

Date

Sunrise

Sunset

Moon phase

Weather (hot, cold, humid, dry, precipitation, clouds, wind etc.)

Signs of the seasons

Sightings/connections (birds, plants, trees, animals, natural features)

Night Sky (stars, constellations, other – meteors, planets etc)

Nature connection activity (what you did, how you felt, what you noticed etc.)

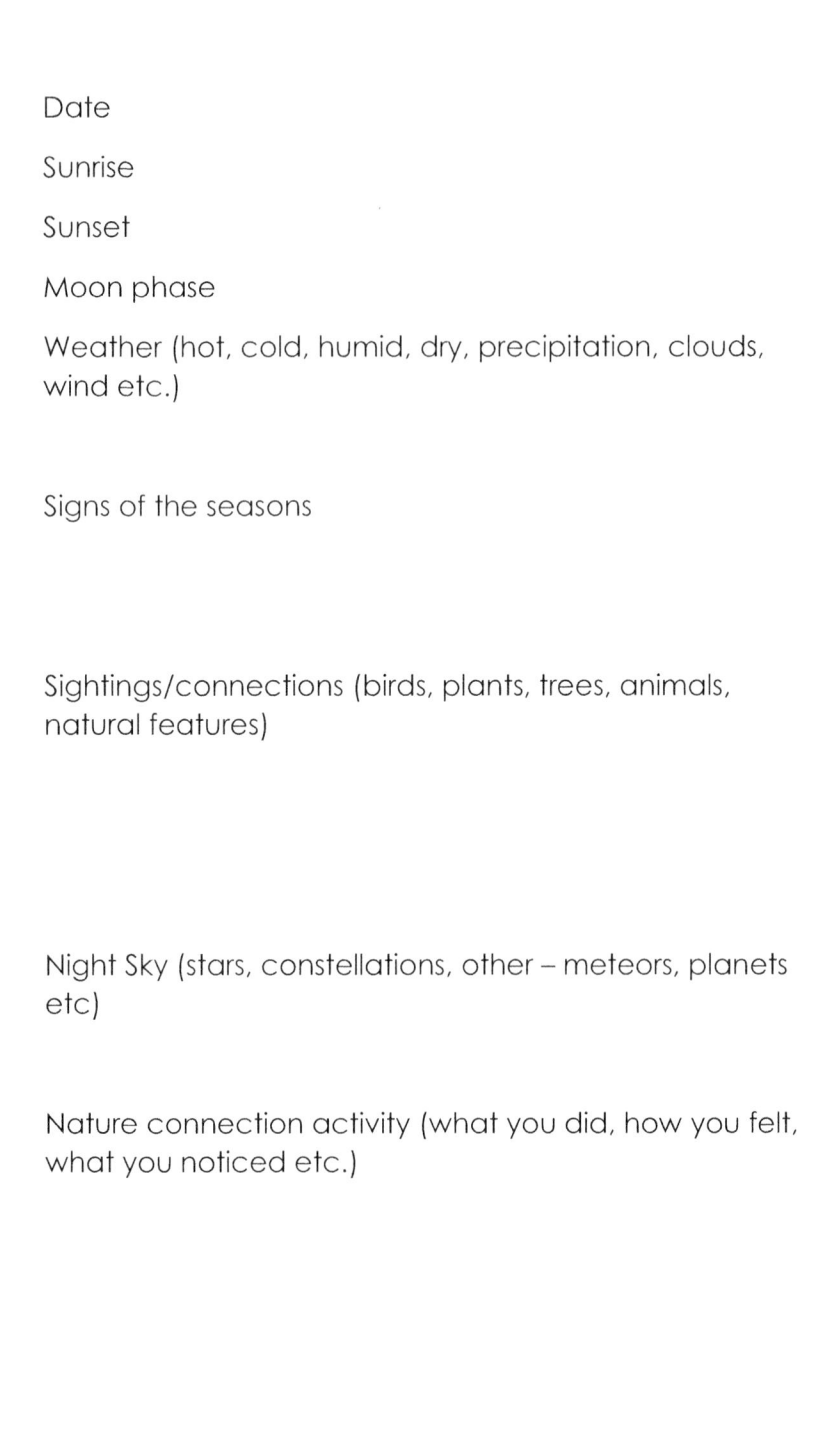

Drawings, pictures, stories, poems, extra notes, gratitudes, ways I gave service to nature

Date

Sunrise

Sunset

Moon phase

Weather (hot, cold, humid, dry, precipitation, clouds, wind etc.)

Signs of the seasons

Sightings/connections (birds, plants, trees, animals, natural features)

Night Sky (stars, constellations, other – meteors, planets etc)

Nature connection activity (what you did, how you felt, what you noticed etc.)

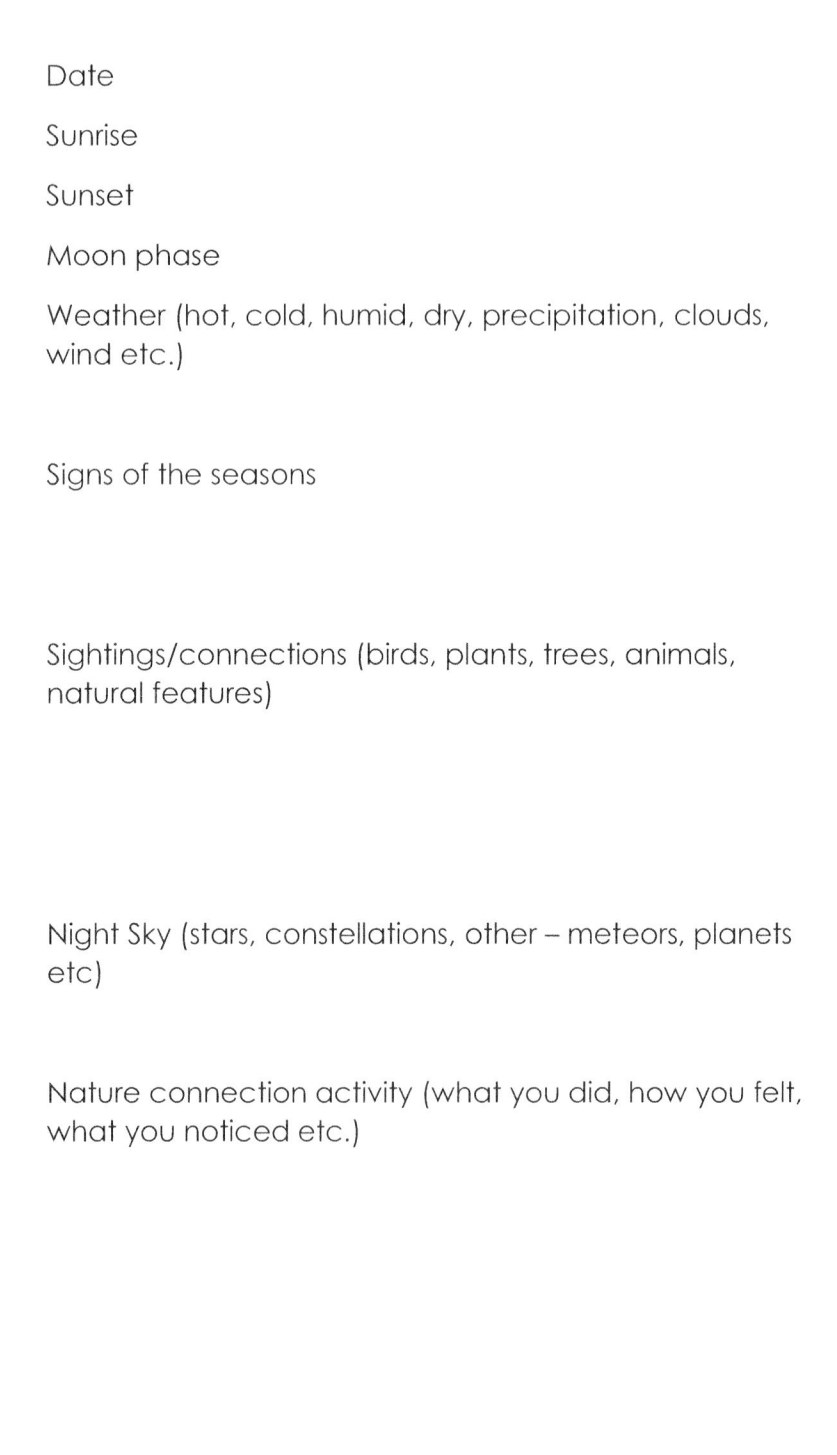

Drawings, pictures, stories, poems, extra notes, gratitudes, ways I gave service to nature

Date

Sunrise

Sunset

Moon phase

Weather (hot, cold, humid, dry, precipitation, clouds, wind etc.)

Signs of the seasons

Sightings/connections (birds, plants, trees, animals, natural features)

Night Sky (stars, constellations, other – meteors, planets etc)

Nature connection activity (what you did, how you felt, what you noticed etc.)

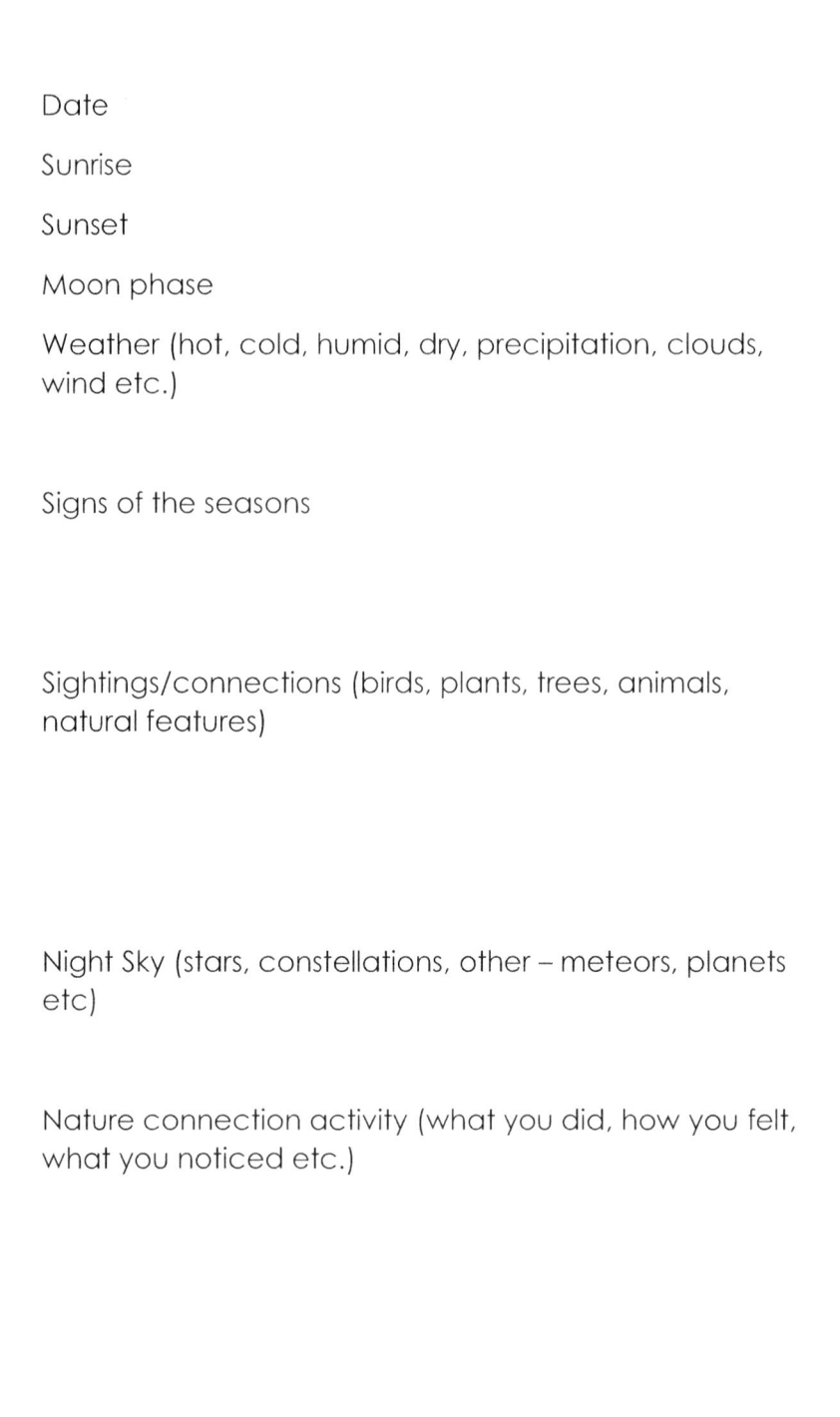

Drawings, pictures, stories, poems, extra notes, gratitudes, ways I gave service to nature

About the Author

Clare Snowdon is a nature connection guide and mindfulness teacher. She founded an online centre at www.dragonmindfulness.co.uk as a way to connect people and share ways to care for one another and the natural world, celebrating compassion and diversity in both humans and non-humans.

Printed in Great Britain
by Amazon